COUGAR BAY
NATURE
PRESERVE

COUGAR BAY NATURE PRESERVE

NATURE PRESERVE

SAVING
COEUR D'ALENE'S
NATURAL GEM

THERESA SHAFFER

THE
History
PRESS

Published by The History Press
Charleston, SC
www.historypress.com

Front cover, bottom, painting by Wes Hanson.

First published 2023

Manufactured in the United States

ISBN 9781467154949

Library of Congress Control Number: 2023937167

Notice: The information in this book is true and complete to the best of our knowledge. It is offered without guarantee on the part of the author or The History Press. The author and The History Press disclaim all liability in connection with the use of this book.

Dedicated to all environmental activists in this great big, beautiful world. I am both humbled and inspired by how you make the seemingly impossible possible. May our children follow their hearts by doing away with fear and replacing it with courage.

But I've learnt that no one is too small to make a difference.
—Greta Thunberg

CONTENTS

FOREWORD

Cougar Bay lies roughly two miles from busy downtown Coeur d'Alene. It is adjacent to the Hagadone Marina on Blackwell Island. Boats speed along Lake Coeur d'Alene's deep water. All this frenzy contrasts with Cougar Bay's relative calm.

Yes, traffic on U.S. 95 roars by the Cougar Bay Nature Preserve heading up and down Mica Hill. But people hiking its trails are quickly absorbed in the bay's natural wonders. They watch insect spirals rising and falling at sunrise and sunset and ospreys hovering. They hear the grating calls of blackbirds in the marsh and chirrs of dragonflies feeding on mosquitoes. If they stand still, they listen to limbs sigh and see sunbathing turtles slide from logs.

Their legs carry them up and down uneven trails where rocks rise like knuckles and roots crisscross boggy places. And when they stop, they can easily conclude Cougar Bay was destined to be a sanctuary. But it was anything but fated. It took deliberate intervention, perseverance and a great deal of good fortune. This book documents what happened on this journey and gives coherence to its sometimes-jumbled events.

Early in the effort, a friend remarked that in the future, people would look at Cougar Bay's preservation as an act of genius. I don't assume this will happen. But diligence, the help of many people and good timing sometimes produce wonderful outcomes.

At Cougar Bay, the stars aligned and gave this community an enduring legacy.

—Wes Hanson

PREFACE

When I retired from the University of Idaho in October 2018, a coworker took me out to lunch to wish me well on my next journey. During our conversation, Juli told me about discovering the Cougar Bay Nature Preserve. She and her husband had lived in Coeur d'Alene for five years and had not known it existed. She was amazed by its hiking trails, its natural setting and especially at how close it was to Coeur d'Alene. Perhaps the lunch was serendipitous. My partner and I had just sorted through old boxes stuffed with newspaper clippings, maps, legal documents and stories from a grueling thirteen-year effort to spare Cougar Bay from development. I told her a few stories I had learned during our clean-out effort. It occurred to me as we talked that I should write the story behind Cougar Bay's preservation. I asked her if she would read a book on the history and preservation of Cougar Bay. My heart wavered, but she was more than enthusiastic about it and urged me to write it.

It has been a long five years since I started researching and writing the Cougar Bay story. However, heartfelt feelings inspire persistence, and I began to visit the preserve more often. Regardless of weather, I met people carrying cameras with large lenses who were excited about taking wildlife photos. I have seen families with children happily walking and running on the trails. Dogs and their owners are often seen on the trails, eager to be out in nature. Waterfowl feed, and birds sing in the marsh. It is a place of constant renewal that, come what may, refreshes our weary souls.

The disappearance of undisturbed open space is not new. It was a concern as far back as 1890 as Euro-Americans spread across America. In north Idaho, the disappearance is alarming. I am both humbled and amazed by the hard work of activists who were tenacious in defending Cougar Bay from further development.

While writing and researching the history of preserving Cougar Bay, I have put my significant other through many iterations, edits and revisions and possibly a little heartache. He didn't particularly want to revisit the thirteen-year battle he and countless others fought to preserve Cougar Bay. He's been faithful to my project, though, and is always ready to answer my never-ending questions. I am utterly grateful to him and to his late wife, Gertie Hanson, who saved "everything." The old boxes of Cougar Bay information contained numerous duplicates of every news account and fundraising event, legal documents and all kinds of correspondences. People who helped with the battle gave them all to Gertie. I send a special thanks to Juli Anderson for her gentle, unknowing inspiration.

The story begins in 1992. It ends in 2005, when the last piece of Cougar Bay property was gifted to the public. Cougar Bay has been through changes since then, mostly aimed at preserving it. This story is an account that involves remarkable timing, persistence and single-minded activism. Hail to endurance, resolve and listening to one's heart. I hope this small book piques your interest in exploring the Cougar Bay Nature Preserve. It, like Tubbs Hill, is a treasure.

ACKNOWLEDGEMENTS

This book could not have happened without the support of my life partner, Wes Hanson. Everything I wrote was read by him and then improved immeasurably by his insights. There are not words enough to thank him for his patience.

I am indebted to the late Scott Reed, who wrote *A Treasure Called Tubbs Hill*, and Mary Lou Reed, who gave me permission to use Scott's essay "Another Winter's Tale," an illuminating account of Cougar Bay once upon a time.

I am deeply grateful to Virginia Johnson, Denise Clark and Dorothy Dahlgren, who read and offered edits and encouraging words for the book in its early stages, and to Shirley Sturts for her expert bird advice and information.

Thank you to the following people and organizations: the Friends of Cougar Bay, Rural Kootenai Organization for your commitment and determination; the Museum of North Idaho and all the amazing work it does to preserve north Idaho's history; E-bird.org for its list of birds identified in Cougar Bay; the Bureau of Land Management for its support and list of plant species; The Nature Conservancy for its support throughout the process of writing this book; Ducks Unlimited for its restoration help at Cougar Bay; the Camera Corral for its expertise; and all the supporters who sent me stories and images. Without their help, I could not have finished this book. And lastly, I want to thank my editor at The History Press, Artie Crisp, who took a chance with me.

CHAPTER 1

THE COUGAR BAY NATURE PRESERVE

In nature nothing exists alone.
—Rachel Carson

Imagine glittering luxury homes forming a necklace surrounding Cougar Bay's shoreline, just two miles southwest of Coeur d'Alene. A dock extends from each home. The once wild bay has been dredged to make canals for noisy boats shuttling to and from the lake. An ornate iron gate blocks the public from entering the development. Waterfowl and secretive wading birds like the great blue heron are gone. Larger forest animals have moved on. These things could easily have occurred. But with remarkable timing and a lengthy battle, they did not.

Instead, golden tamaracks glow in autumn. Woolly bear caterpillars, harbingers of winter, inch their way across hiking trails. Red-winged blackbirds bob on cattails, while painted turtles sunbathe on logs. A red-tailed hawk's *kee-arh* cry triggers frantic quacking from cinnamon teal ducks. You can hike on a well-worn trail that weaves along the bay's shoreline. A well-placed bench under the shade of an old cottonwood tree is a place where someone can reflect or rest. Despite the nearby highway hum, you sense this is very much a place of renewal and resilience.

Cougar Bay is a shallow water body located at the northwest corner of Lake Coeur d'Alene. The lake is 25 miles long and 10 miles across at its widest point, with an average depth of about 100 feet. The lake was once described by *National Geographic* magazine as one of the five

A bench sponsored by The Nature Conservancy under a cottonwood tree. *Author's collection.*

most beautiful lakes in the world. The Cougar Bay Nature Preserve lies protected in the southwest area of the bay. As you drive north on U.S. 95, the preserve serves as a gateway into the city of Coeur d'Alene. At any time of the year, you will see a rich variety of wildlife and an ever-changing landscape at the nature preserve. In fact, the *Idaho Wildlife Viewing Guide*

Cougar Bay trail. *The Nature Conservancy photo.*

states that the Cougar Bay Nature Preserve is one of the best wildlife-viewing sites in Idaho. Locals or weary travelers just needing a respite wander its trails, which encompasses over 2.2 miles of hiking trails, 243.51 acres of forestland and more than 6,800 feet of shoreline. Cougar Bay and its shoreline attract many kinds of fish, marsh birds, raptors, turtles and a menagerie of waterfowl to its shallow water.

Springtime brings ducklings trailing their mothers across U.S. 95 to the bay. Tundra swans stop to feed on their migration north. Ospreys nest and raise their young on pilings once used to corral logs. During spring migrations, the bay fills with waterfowl, including Canada geese and a variety of ducks. Their noisy and often raucous activities are a birdwatcher's delight. As spring begins, the bay's water rises to its natural level because of melting snow. This free flow continues until typically the end of June, depending on the snowpack and weather. Once spring runoff flows recede and diminished flows are forecast, Avista (formerly Washington Water Power Company) closes spill gates at its Post Falls Dam. This closure begins to fill the nine-mile stretch of the Spokane River and Lake Coeur d' Alene, including Cougar Bay.

In the summer, osprey can be seen diving from a tall tree or log piling into the lake, emerging with a fish writhing in their talons. Some of the birds migrating to the lake for the summer include great blue herons, spotted sandpipers, common snipes, mountain bluebirds, violet-green swallows, cinnamon teal ducks and pied-billed and western grebes. Birdwatchers and photographers gather near the bay to observe and record their sightings.

In fall's pre-dawn light, hunters park along the highway shoulder. They trek down to the Bureau of Land Management's eleven-acre public shoreline at Cougar Bay's north side. As nervous ducks and geese swim from them, the hunters rise from their makeshift hunting blinds with their dogs and fire shotgun pellets into erupting wings.

In late December, due to its shallowness, Cougar Bay sometimes freezes over and forms a natural ice-skating rink. Ice skating and ice fishing are still local pleasurable pastimes. The region used to experience frigid winters that froze over Lake Coeur d'Alene's bays and smaller surrounding lakes for weeks. In the twenty-first century, we are lucky if Cougar Bay freezes over enough for a few days of exciting outdoor pursuits. On those icy winter days, ice fishermen venture out and sit beside glowing fires hoping to attract curious fish and brave skaters try their skills on the ice. To further realize the beauty and romance of Cougar Bay, you may want to read the late Scott Reed's essay "Another Winter's Tale" in Appendix A. Scott's essay is a tribute to the winter splendor of a time gone by, especially on Cougar Bay and nearby Fernan Lake. Scott Reed, an outdoor enthusiast and environmental lawyer, was a regular contributor to the local free paper, *The Nickels Worth*. Reed wrote a similar book to this one called *A Treasure Called Tubbs Hill*. Tubbs Hill is a nature sanctuary adjacent to downtown Coeur d'Alene.

The effort to preserve Cougar Bay began with concerned citizens in 1992. Then, it was only a dream. It all started with a housing development proposal that stirred determined opposition. The conflict involved numerous public hearings, costly legal actions and land purchases over a period of thirteen years. Remarkably, most of Cougar Bay's shore was preserved as public land by an improbable combination of determined local activists, a Hawaiian developer, a cantankerous Cougar Bay landowner, Kootenai County, the Bureau of Land Management (BLM), Crown Pacific Lumber Company and The Nature Conservancy (TNC). The dream came true in 2005. The phrase "Sometimes it takes a village" could not be more apt. This preserve is the legacy left to us, a landscape filled with nature's vibrancy, tenaciously fought for by advocates who understood its worth. Private lake homes were denied on Cougar Bay. This was and is unusual on a lake where the shoreline is more than 90 percent privately owned.

Geology of Cougar Bay

Lake Coeur d'Alene, like other surrounding lakes, was formed by the Missoula floods. The Missoula floods (also known as the Spokane floods) were catastrophic glacial lake outburst floods that swept periodically across north Idaho and eastern Washington at the end of the last ice age. Lake

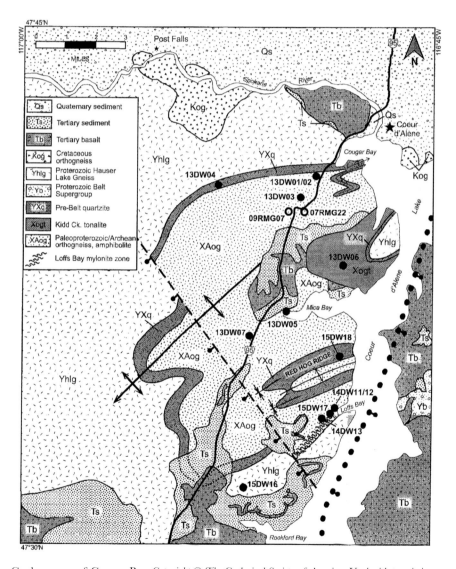

Geology map of Cougar Bay. *Copyright © The Geological Society of America. Used with permission.*

19

Coeur d'Alene was not gouged out by the glacial floods. Rather, it was formed when the flood's gravel outwash blocked the old St. Joe River basin and its water rose. When the new lake overflowed, it created a new channel in this gravel and formed the Spokane River. It flows to the Post Falls Dam, where it drops down to the original St. Joe River bed.

Reed Lewis, from the Idaho Geological Survey at the University of Idaho, states that "the quartzite [metamorphosed sandstone—YXq on map] within the Cougar Bay Nature Preserve is quite important from a geologic perspective. It rests on top of some of the oldest rocks in Idaho (2.6 and 1.86 billion years old and referred to as 'basement rocks'). The basement rocks are exposed along the U.S. 95 Mica Hill roadcuts. Above quartzite is the Belt Supergroup, metamorphosed sedimentary rocks that are about 1.46 billion years old. This relationship was only discovered in 2012."

An abstract, "A Geological Study of Cougar Bay," was done in collaboration with several colleges and universities[1] (see Appendix F). The map of the area has been provided by the Geological Society of America.

GEOGRAPHY OF COUGAR BAY

Geology underpins geography. Cougar Bay's uniqueness is that it is a wetland with easy access from the city of Coeur d'Alene. The south side of the bay remains wild and untouched, providing diverse habitat for wildlife breeding, nesting and raising young.

Cougar Bay has steep forested hills rising to the northwest and southeast. Cougar Creek flows into Cougar Bay from the west. The bay is about one square mile in area with a depth of between six and seven feet. The watershed area is about eight miles long and two and a half miles wide. Snowmelt carries some sediment into the bay. This process has been taking place for some twenty thousand years. Over the past one hundred years, this process has accelerated because of nearby human-driven development, farming practices and logging.

Water erodes steep hillsides and meanders through bottomland soil to the bay. These nutrients plus decomposing plants fertilize its thick marsh and promote aquatic growth. This soil is a rich mixture of broken-down rock, decayed plants and, to some extent, volcanic ash. As a result, nearby hay farming prospers. Song and wading birds, amphibians and fish love these habitats. Wild turkeys, deer, moose and occasional beavers use shoreline riparian areas. Grass-like vegetation—rushes, sedges, cattails and grasses—grow in and around depressions and mounds in the wetland. Douglas fir and larch thrive on the bay's shaded south side, while on its sunny north side, Ponderosa pines dominate.[2]

CHAPTER 2

A SHORT HISTORY OF COUGAR BAY

The Earth does not belong to us; we belong to the Earth.
—*Chief Seattle*

THE GATHERING PLACE

As with all land in America, the land around Cougar Bay and the bay itself were once unowned. The Coeur d'Alene Indians were once stewards of the entire lake. They cared for it, used it for their survival and passed along oral stories connected to the lake. They gathered in the area where Lake Coeur d'Alene flows into the Spokane River, near the North Idaho College grounds and what is now Cougar Bay. The Coeur d'Alene called this area *Hnya'(p qi'nn* (pronounced "hin-yap-keehn-un"), or the "gathering place." It was a busy place, especially in the summer, when the Coeur d'Alene gathered to fish, dance, feast and swim. The lake was named after the Coeur d'Alene people, a federally recognized tribe of Native Americans who refer to themselves as Schitsu'umsh, which translates to "the ones that were found here." Coeur d'Alene, which means "Heart of an Awl," comes from French-Canadian fur traders. The traders apparently found the Indians to be shrewd traders. The Coeur d'Alene reservation is currently located near Plummer, Idaho, which is roughly thirty-five miles south of Coeur d'Alene's downtown area.

Life changed for the Northwest Native Americans as pioneers started to move west seeking gold and silver in the mid-1800s. There were many skirmishes with the Indians. The Coeur d'Alene War of 1858 ultimately

Coeur d'Alene Indian Village, circa 1890. Overview looking across the Spokane River at Fort Sherman from Blackwell Hill in winter. Indian tepees are in the foreground on Blackwell Island. *Museum of North Idaho.*

ended the local Indian wars. When Congress established Idaho as a territory in 1863, it separated Coeur d'Alene Indian territory from the state, including lakes and rivers. At that time, all of Lake Coeur d'Alene lay within the Coeur d'Alene Indian territory. In 1873, President Ulysses S. Grant established the Coeur d'Alene Indian Reservation by executive order, reducing its land to 600,000 acres. The Coeur d'Alene Indians resented being moved to a federal reservation, and the War Department feared an uprising. Consequently, Fort Sherman was established in 1878 near the original site of an Indian village and trading post built in 1813. In 1889, the Coeur d'Alene Indians ceded property encompassing the upper two-thirds of the lake to the U.S. government.[3] Fort Sherman was abandoned in 1901. Three of the original fort buildings still exist within what is now the North Idaho College grounds, including the Fort Sherman chapel, Coeur d'Alene's oldest church. The "little red chapel" was gifted to the Museum of North Idaho. After much-needed restoration, it is typically used as an event venue.

Ed Johnson, whose family once owned 118 acres above Cougar Bay, stated that his grandfather used to trade with the Coeur d'Alene Indians in the 1930s through 1940s. The Coeur d'Alene would drive north from the

The little red chapel, Fort Sherman Chapel, 1975. *Museum of North Idaho.*

Plummer area and stop at the cottonwood tree grove that lined Cougar Bay. They came by horse and buggy in the summer to pick huckleberries near Hayden Lake, which lies about eight miles north of Coeur d'Alene. On their way back home, they stopped at the cottonwood grove. Ed's grandfather traded them cream and grain for huckleberries.

Today, because the Coeur d'Alene Reservation surrounds the lower one-third of the lake, the lakebed and banks in that area belong to the tribe. In 1992, the Coeur d'Alene filed a federal lawsuit that asserted the State of Idaho had no rights or interests in the lower one-third of lakebed and banks. In 2001, the U.S. Supreme Court ruled the Coeur d'Alene tribe owned Lake Coeur d'Alene south of Harrison. The rest of the lake and the lake bottom, including Cougar Bay, is held in public trust by the State of Idaho.

The Meadows

In the late 1800s, a handful of homesteaders occupied Cougar Bay, which was then known as the Meadows. Hay fields extended out to where the pilings and the Hagadone Marina are now located, at Lake Coeur d'Alene's outlet to the Spokane River. In this area, the shallow bay drops into deeper Lake Coeur d'Alene. The bay gradually becomes shallower as you move southwest toward the Cougar Bay Nature Preserve parking lot. In 1906, the Washington Water Power hydroelectric dam on the Spokane River at Post Falls began operating to provide power for local industries. By 1907, flooding caused by the dam had inundated the Meadows, thus forming Cougar Bay.

Portions of present-day Cougar Bay were originally homesteaded by J.P. Healy, Samuel Amsler, James Graham and John Wells. We will focus on J.P. Healy's land, as this is the property later sold to the Hawaiian developer that initiated the struggle to save Cougar Bay from development. In June 1894, J.P. Healy made claim to 160 acres in the present-day Cougar Bay area "for the purpose of actual settlement and cultivation." The Healy family fenced in about 80 acres of Cougar Bay's hay meadow, where they regularly cut and sold hay. The wild hay (meadow grass) was a major feed for cattle and milk cows in the winter. On October 12, 1907, after the first full summer of the Post Falls Dam's operation, the *Coeur d'Alene Press* published an article describing farming in the Meadows. The photograph depicting several cows standing in the then-flooded Healy land is blurry, but the accompanying article describes the photo's content:

> *The picture accompanying this article shows the meadows of J.P. Healy under water as a result of the high dam which the Washington Water Power Company (WWP) built at Post Falls.*
>
> *Where the cattle are standing to their bodies* [sic] *was once a fine meadow from which Mr. Healy cut many tons of hay for winter forage for*

The Post Falls Dam with a boy and a man looking over the falls, circa 1945. *Museum of North Idaho.*

The Meadows on Cougar Bay. *Museum of North Idaho, June 15, 1909.*

his cattle. By the act of the water-power company this fine dairy farm is ruined and made a watery waste. It is three feet under [water] in many places and the company has created in Coeur d'Alene Lake the largest storage [water] reservoir in the world.

This image of Cougar Bay is from the Samuel Amsler homestead looking southwest. John M. Elder had a homestead along Cougar Bay. The photographer was his son Paul Elder. Written on the envelope was, "Overlooking meadows from Amsler Hill," now known as Blackwell Hill.

After it flooded Healy's homestead in 1907, WWP undertook a survey to determine the amount of Healy's hay field that had been "rendered absolutely valueless." WWP calculated that 93.2 acres of Healy's homestead was below the recognized 2,128-foot-high water mark and purchased an easement to flood these acres for the princely sum of $4,750.

The remaining unflooded area included a large grove of cottonwood trees along the waterside edge of U.S. 95 that extended to Cougar Creek. Cougar Bay was mostly under water, but this area continued to be hayed until 1943. Because of the great need for power during World War II, the Washington Water Power Company raised the water level at its Post Falls Dam. Doing this increased Lake Coeur d'Alene's water level. Haying was impossible after that.

Over the years, the Healys sold pieces of the property, keeping 11.6 acres and 3,100 feet of shoreline and 20 acres across the highway from the bay. This upland area became the present-day Cougar Bay Estates. By and large, WWP's Post Falls Dam created Cougar Bay.

COUGAR BAY PILINGS AND THE INFLUENCE OF LUMBER MILLS

Following an 1898 report made by a U.S. Geological Survey about the abundant timber resources in the Pacific Northwest, several eastern lumber companies moved into north Idaho and began building their empires. These companies purchased vast amounts of timberlands and built mills, railroads, logging camps, company stores and even town sites. With the logging boom in full swing by 1910, thousands of people swarmed into north Idaho, swelling the population of Coeur d'Alene to more than seven thousand. Lumber mills abounded in the early twentieth century along the Spokane River and Lake Coeur d'Alene.

CHAPTER 3

COUGAR BAY'S HABITATS
AND CREATURES

All good things are wild and free.
—Henry David Thoreau

THE WETLAND CALLED COUGAR BAY

A wetland is not just a wet area. It needs to have three components, and water is only one of these. The other two are hydrophytes (water-loving plants) and hydric soils. Wetland plants are unique in that they like to be saturated and live in anaerobic environments. The two major types of hydric soils are mineral and organic. If the water table fluctuates, as it does in Cougar Bay, the soil is mottled and may be hydric. The most dynamic wetlands are marshes and riparian areas, like Cougar Bay. They are associated with flowing water and flooding.

Cougar Bay has been a marsh wetland with a floodplain riparian area since what was once meadowland was flooded out by the Washington Water Power dam. In Idaho, wetlands also include riparian areas, green zones of vegetation between the water's edge and the start of upland plants. Cougar Bay's wetland fits this definition. Riparian areas sustain many types of plants and provide travel corridors for animals.

More than 75 percent of Idaho's wild species depend on wetlands during their life cycle. Wetlands, however, make up only 1 percent of America's land. The shade and vegetation in a wetland provide cooler waters and insects for fish. Dense vegetation and slow-moving water improve water quality. Compact wetland root systems help keep banks stabilized when threatened by flooding. Wetlands are the foundation for the transfer of energy. Plants turn energy into food for animals to eat and are eaten in turn. Nearly 50 percent of bird species rely on wetland and riparian habitats. These habitats support numerous game and fish species (from native trout and waterfowl to moose and beaver), as well as up to 50 percent of Idaho's wildlife and rare plants.[5] These benefits are among many reasons why Cougar Bay's conservation is so important.

OSPREYS, COUGARS, OH MY!

Many ospreys inhabit Cougar Bay. The Idaho Panhandle is home to more than two hundred pairs of ospreys, making it one of the largest populations in the western United States. Often called fish hawks, ospreys are a distinct species among birds of prey. They have flexible front and back talons, which allow them to grasp. Rough, wart-like nodules on their feet help them hold on to flailing fish. Their breathtaking feet-first plunge to pluck fish out of shallow waters is spectacular to behold. In a 2017 article in the *Spokesman Review*, biologist Wayne Melquist said, "Over the past two decades I have seen between 3–15 osprey pairs nest in Cougar Bay every year. The pilings are ideal locations to nest as food is just a dive away."

Melquist has been banding juvenile ospreys in north Idaho for more than forty years. The long-running research project offers important insight into the lives of these impressive birds, which raise their young on northern lakes and rivers but winter in Mexico and Central America. Melquist's work has helped increase our understanding of nesting patterns, migration routes, population densities and interchange with other osprey populations. Each band is marked with an identification code and a phone number for people to call when they find a dead bird. The data goes into a national registry for research.

When Melquist started banding in the early 1970s, ospreys and other raptor populations were threatened by the pesticide DDT, which caused their eggshells to break. A ban on DDT use in the United States has led to a rebound in bird populations. Nowadays, most of the threats to north Idaho's ospreys are human-caused. Fishing line, which can get tangled in their nests and talons, is a common peril, as are oblivious fishermen fishing too close to osprey nests.

The Cougar Bay Osprey Protective Association has maintained forty-four existing pilings since 2013. Twenty-two of them provide goose-proof nesting platforms for their stick-built nests. Feeding male ospreys use the remaining pilings as resting places. These are safe perches and a welcome refuge for ospreys.

Once a year, the public can view ospreys in their nests during a cruise on the *Mish-n-Nock* boat in July. The cruise is sponsored by the Coeur d'Alene Regional Chamber of Commerce. The Coeur d'Alene tribe originated the cruise to raise awareness of the ospreys' plight, and they usually have a tribal member on board. The two-decked boat travels near Cougar Bay's pilings and booms. Wildlife experts on ospreys and other species provide information and answer questions to help cruise attendees learn more about these iconic north Idaho and Lake Coeur d'Alene birds. Other birds often seen include cormorants and many varieties of ducks and grebes.

Bald eagles also can be spotted overlooking the protected bay. Some nesting pairs remain year-round near Lake Coeur d'Alene, although most bald eagles in Idaho are migratory. From November to February, they feed on spawning kokanee salmon in Wolf Lodge Bay in Lake Coeur d'Alene. Wolf Lodge Bay is seven miles southeast of Coeur d'Alene. After the fish spawn, they die and float to the surface of the water, creating an abundant source of food for the eagles. Eagle watching during these months has become increasingly popular. Photographers and onlookers can get close enough to see the birds perched on trees, diving for the dead fish or soaring above the bay.[6]

Game Animals and Special Species at Cougar Bay

The Bureau of Land Management (BLM) made an environmental assessment in 2014 to construct a one-mile hiking trail at the nature preserve. It found evidence of elk, deer, moose and wild turkey use on the site. The low elevation and proximity to water were ideal for waterfowl and many other wildlife species. The project site also provided habitat, food and abundant cover for mountain lions, bear, grouse, bobcats and various small mammal species. In addition, Cougar Bay supplied habitat for special status species, such as the Coeur d'Alene salamander, the northern alligator lizard and numerous bats.

Westslope cutthroat trout, a BLM sensitive species, are found in Lake Coeur d'Alene and many of its tributaries, including Cougar Creek and Cougar Bay. Westslope cutthroat trout stock exist at very low levels due to degradation of their habitat, mostly caused by mining, logging and development. Overfishing and the introduction of nonnative species also contributed to their reduced numbers. The BLM concluded the planned trail would not affect the fish because only a short section of the proposed trail would be within about one hundred feet of Cougar Bay; the rest of the trail heads up the hillside away from the water.

THE SOUND OF A COUGAR

The place names Cougar Gulch and Cougar Bay have legendary and historic origins. The gulch reportedly got its name from the number of mountain lions killed there during the Fort Sherman days. Local lore has it that the name "Cougar Gulch" was given by a soldier from Fort Sherman who shot a cougar there.

By all accounts, cougars were numerous and a common sight prior to a 1910 wildfire. They posed a constant threat to livestock. Because of housing developments, hunting and fewer wildlife corridors in the area, the cougar population has declined. Yet stories of cougar sightings still abound.

In 1910, a wildfire swept through Cougar Gulch, wiping out many cougars, according to local people. The fire was part of the regional big burn. The dry summer heat increased the fire danger. Numerous fires were burning throughout the region and eventually burned more than three million acres of timber in north Idaho and northwest Montana. On August 20, hurricane-force winds combined them into a conflagration. While most accounts focus on the Silver Valley, where the town of Wallace was mostly burned down, fires raged near Coeur d'Alene too. On that same day, a big fire burning on Mica Peak drifted over the mountain toward Cougar Gulch. One Cougar

A cougar. *Courtesy of Idaho Fish and Game.*

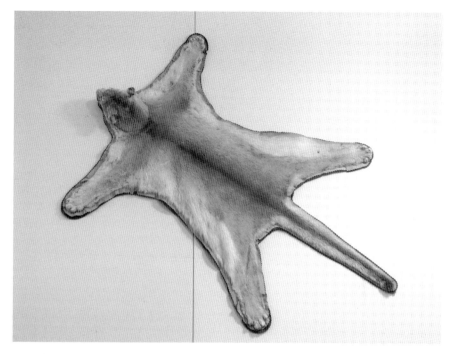

A cougar skin rug. *Author's collection.*

Gulch resident, Marie Blocksom, wrote that her father fought the fire for four days and nights with only an hour of sleep but finally stopped it before it reached his buildings. The family had packed everything it could and was ready to put it all in their wagon and flee if the fire continued.

In 1971, Sadie Brooten, a writer and local historian, wrote an article for the *Coeur d'Alene Press* recalling stories from families who lived in Cougar Gulch before and after the infamous fire. Brooten stated that the exact year of the naming is unknown, but an 1888 forestry map identifies both the gulch and the bay as Cougar Gulch and Cougar Bay.

Brooten interviewed Mrs. James O'Reilly, who lived in the Gulch until 1924. She recalled:

> *It was a wild place in those days. There were lots of cougars, coyotes, bear, deer and other wild animals and we always kept the gun on a rack above the door. One day a cougar was prowling around in back of the house after the calves and Mr. O'Reilly went and shot him. He's a "big fella," 12 feet long or more. We skinned him and made a cougar rug which we used for a good many years.*

Another story that circulates is that one day, a cougar was seen swimming in the bay. When it reached one of the log pilings, it began to climb to an osprey nest. Whether the cat caught the osprey or its fledglings is unknown. There is a painting of this incident by artist Kelly Meyer, but no one knows its whereabouts.

Along with other residents, I have had my own experience. My encounter with a local cougar came one evening as I was camped in the meadow on our property above Cougar Bay. As dusk settled upon us, I heard bawling that sounded like a baby. It was extremely unsettling and very eerie. I had never heard such a sound. The noise came from an overgrown brushy and treed area a short distance from our tent. After listening a while, I told my partner I was going to check it out. He grabbed my ankle as I was exiting the tent and said, "Better not. Sounds like a cougar." The bawling gradually faded. We didn't leave the tent until dawn.

CHAPTER 4

CHANGE COMES TO COUGAR BAY

1992

The eyes of the future are looking back at us,
and they are praying for us to see beyond our own time.
—Terry Tempest Williams

Cougar Bay sat for decades without any further development because a sizable portion of the south end was privately owned. The owner, John Pointer, was not interested in development and basically took care of the submerged bay by creating canals throughout it. Another Cougar Bay shoreline owner, the Healy family, had not developed their shoreline property either. Part of the Healys' property comprised 11.6 acres of dry land with 3,100 feet of shoreline and about 80 acres of submerged property. Nevertheless, in January 1992, Mary Ellen Weber, an heir to Ignatius Healy (J.P. Healy's son), sold the Healy property on the north end of Cougar Bay to Hawaiian developer Mike McCormack.

The *Coeur d'Alene Press* soon announced that a Hawaiian developer had purchased shoreline and submerged land on Cougar Bay. The newspaper said a seven-lot subdivision was being proposed for the strip of shore land between the highway and bay. The project was christened with an idealistic name, "Cougar Beach." "Cougar Beach would have little impact on the bay," said the developer, "and would even protect the bay from further human encroachment." Ironically, the proposed development threatened to significantly alter the shoreline's natural qualities. A natural place like Cougar Bay influences the viewpoints and values of people living near

Healy shoreline. *Author's collection.*

it. The developer did not consider the local public's strong attachment to Cougar Bay. Activists quickly stepped up to save it from turning into a picturesque backdrop for a residential development. A long and successful battle began.

McCormack organized as McCormack Properties of Idaho. In addition to the shoreline, he purchased approximately twenty acres upland from the Healy family. It is now the gated Cougar Bay Estates development.

In 1992, Coeur d'Alene's legal area of city impact was one mile from the city's border. The Healy property was just beyond its border. In spite of this, a meeting was set up by the developer with the city to describe the development proposal. A few concerned citizens who heard about the development plan went to the City of Coeur d'Alene Planning and Zoning Commission meeting to hear about the plan. They expressed worry that the proposed development would impact environmentally sensitive Cougar Bay. This commission raised no concerns, and the proposal was passed on to the city council.

A few weeks later, the city council heard from eleven citizens, including a local bird expert, who opposed the project. However, the city council

Cougar Bay Estates gate. *Author's collection.*

Mike McCormack. *Courtesy of the* Spokesman Review.

supported the subdivision proposal unanimously. The developer claimed Cougar Beach would actually complement the bay's ecology by stabilizing the northern shore's land use and eliminating the duck hunting that threatened waterfowl.[7] He did not mention that it would triple the number of people living there, enrich the water with fertilizer runoff and eventually lead to demands that the bay be dredged for boat access. However, the city's endorsement of the subdivision concept was only symbolic since Cougar Bay's shoreline was not in the city's jurisdiction. The concerned citizens left dejected, wondering what to do. The interval between this perfunctory review and the legal hearing before the county would provide time for people to organize against the project.

THE FRIENDS OF COUGAR BAY

The city's nonbinding approval roused a dedicated group of activists to form the Friends of Cougar Bay, also known as the Friends. They were led by their belief that preserving natural areas like Cougar Bay made good sense for wildlife and the community. The Friends members threw themselves into a pitched battle to stop development on the bay. They began researching and contacting public agencies. The first thing they found was that the land was inappropriately zoned. Five homes—not seven, as proposed by McCormack—could be built per acre within twenty-five feet of the shoreline. The Friends found that the subdivision's fertilizer runoff would negatively affect Cougar Bay's water quality and that more than half the property was in the floodplain. As information accumulated, they learned how some developers work and public agencies often respond. Developers provide minimal facts and figures that favor their projects. Piecemeal presentations thwart attempts by agencies and the public to see their projects in total. Public agencies often receive the developer's barrage of information in bulk just before scheduled hearings, so they are pressured to approve permits without thoughtful review. But the Friends' vision of a healthy, publicly owned Cougar Bay sustained them, despite growing exasperation with a public hearing process that promoted careless development.

After spending weeks organizing opposition to McCormack Properties' proposal, the Friends of Cougar Bay went public by gathering 2,500 signatures at the Kootenai County Fair in early August 1992. On Tuesday, August 11, the Friends of Cougar Bay held a public meeting at the Mica Grange Hall. The Friends vowed to fight developer Mike McCormack's plans for the seven-home development on one of the last pristine bays on Lake Coeur d'Alene. McCormack, who lived near the Grange on Tall Pines Road, did not attend the meeting. But his attorney, Mike Newell, did. Newell said there would be a subdivision on the bay whether people wanted one or not: "That property's going to be developed, if not today, tomorrow." The opponents said they wanted time to study the proposed development and raise money if needed to buy the property so that it could remain a scenic viewing and wildlife area. Wes Hanson, the meeting's organizer, stated that if the seven-home waterfront subdivision was built, it would not take long for homes to line the remainder of the bay. "It is really one of the only places on the lake where a person has a sense of what the lake gives to us," he said. Hanson also said local land-use ordinances and permit-granting agencies failed to contemplate the full impact of a development like McCormack's. Attorney Newell countered that he, too, was a "friend of Cougar Bay" but said that if the opponents attempted to block the development, they would have no influence on how it was built. This intimidation tactic did not sit well with the Friends.[8]

On August 16, 1992, the group organized a flotilla of about twenty boats on Cougar Bay to support the bay's preservation as a wildlife refuge. The Friends hauled along newspaper reporters. Blustery winds drove the boats apart in the bay and shredded one of two banners. Despite the weather, the Friends managed to string a large banner that read "SAVE COUGAR BAY" in between two log pilings. The protest got the attention of the community, the county commissioners and the city council members, temporarily stalling the development. The Friends kept the

Save Cougar Bay flotilla. *Courtesy of the* Spokesman Review.

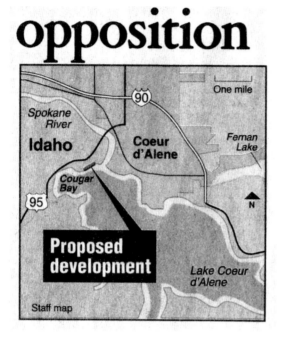

Opposition map. *Courtesy of the Spokesman Review.*

momentum going, becoming even more tenacious in exploring a means to stop shoreline development on Cougar Bay.

After the token city public meetings, the development plan finally came before the county. Some three hundred people crowded into the public hearing. Most of them opposed the subdivision. The developer and his supporters walked in wearing slogan-plastered buttons and carrying American flags. They championed private property rights and the merits of the project. In one misguided statement, the developer's lawyer said that in his home state of Minnesota, wildlife actually sought human company. The audience was dumbfounded; wildlife in Idaho must indeed be peculiar. After four hours, the meeting was discontinued and rescheduled. No one had been allowed to testify in opposition, and close to three hundred enraged people stalked out.

The Friends soon discovered that the U.S. Bureau of Land Management had money coming from a land exchange that could be used to purchase the shoreline property. However, the BLM said it had earmarked the money for other projects in north Idaho and firmly rejected the Friends of Cougar Bay's request. Once again, the Friends persisted, sending out letters and gaining support from a congressional representative and influential community members. The BLM rejection turned into a tentative maybe.

One of the members of the Friends was lawyer Scott Reed, who contacted The Idaho Nature Conservancy (TNC). The Conservancy sometimes provided immediate funding for the outright purchase of land to protect natural places and would later sell it to government agencies. In Idaho, TNC has been active since the mid-1960s and opened the Idaho Field Office in Sun Valley in 1986. Unlike activist environmental organizations that use lobbying and lawsuits, TNC uses only negotiation, compromise and hard cash to accomplish its goals. This possibility appealed to the Friends, who had exhausted other options. The group had already unmasked the project's flaws, enlisted public support and brought the development to a standstill. The Nature Conservancy and Scott Reed negotiated with the developer while the Friends of Cougar Bay waited with hope through the fall of 1992.

The Nature Conservancy

Finally, in March 1993, The Idaho Nature Conservancy asked to meet with the Friends of Cougar Bay at Scott Reed's office. The Friends learned that the developer would sell his shore land at a reduced assessed market value to TNC. The one caveat imposed by McCormack's attorney was that the

Cougar Bay view. *The Nature Conservancy.*

Friends of Cougar Bay as an organization would not oppose McCormack Properties' development plan for a recently purchased adjacent 118 acres overlooking the bay. On this property, McCormack would soon propose building a ninety-two-home subdivision called the Ridge at Cougar Bay. It would be located on the hillside above Cougar Bay, west of U.S. 95. At that meeting, the Friends and their supporters were stunned. Very few of the Friends wanted to promote this or any other development around the bay, though some said it was the bay's preservation they were seeking all along. After a vote, most of the Friends agreed to remain neutral and accept the developer's offer. This decision effectively silenced the Friends but saved a prime piece of Cougar Bay's shoreline. The group dissolved shortly after this decision.

In April 1994, The Nature Conservancy acquired the first parcel of key habitat in Cougar Bay, the former Healy shoreline, for $500,000 from McCormack Properties. It had been appraised at approximately $920,000. The Nature Conservancy functioned as an intermediary for the BLM until federal funds became available.

The Bureau of Land Management

This agreement was and is a landmark compromise between a lakeshore developer and those who fought to protect the bay from overdevelopment. Activists fought and won. However, this was just the beginning of a ten-year battle to save the rest of the largely wild, untouched bay.

The BLM had funds earmarked for north Idaho, now including the Cougar Bay wetland. The money came from a controversial land swap begun in 1992 between the BLM and Potlatch Corporation. It was called the Arkansas-Idaho Land Exchange. Part of the agreement included funding of the Idaho Lands Project, which called for acquisition of lake access and wetlands.[9] Under the Arkansas-Idaho land exchange legislation, sensitive wetlands owned by Potlatch Corporation in Arkansas were traded to the federal government (Bureau of Land Management) in exchange for twenty thousand acres of timberland in north Idaho. To reach parity, $20 million was supposed to be given to the BLM.

As it turned out, the BLM received only a portion of the pledged funds. Nonetheless, a portion of the appropriations that were finally negotiated would be earmarked for acquisition of wetlands in Lake Coeur d'Alene's Cougar Bay and other land around the lake. In the late spring of 1994, ownership of the former Healy parcel was transferred to the Bureau of Land Management for long-term management.

The BLM held a meeting in July 1994 to hear public input and present ideas on managing its newly purchased Cougar Bay shoreline property. According to Ted Graf, the BLM public relations officer, there were two stipulations on the use of the Cougar Bay parcel: (1) wildlife viewing and (2) environmental educational opportunities. Graf proposed that the area would be suitable for a small parking area, an interpretive center where displays would be set up, a trail leading down to the shoreline and a primitive fishing dock. More than a few attendees voiced their concerns on the impact of a fishing dock and any trails leading down to the lake. One attendee, Dale Beeks, a representative of the Citizens for Responsible Growth, felt that "the impact of fishing [wouldn't] work." He said some people burned tires on the beach to attract catfish. Several other people voiced concerns that the waterfowl nesting in the marshy area would be disturbed by a trail. Another person stated that with only 2 percent of the lake being accessible to the public, the parcel could be used to address a recreational need for a boat launch and campsite. At the meeting, The Nature Conservancy stressed that the primary goal should be to protect the wetlands while still providing wildlife viewing. Later, in 1996, McCormack suggested to the BLM that it put a dock on the former Healy shoreline and even allow his development to draw water from the lake for him to use later. Neither suggestion was pursued.[10]

Today, the parcel is rather hidden. A chain-link fence with a small gate protects it from vehicle access and large watercraft being launched from the shoreline. A tree-shrouded sign states that the BLM manages this parcel but contains little information on its uses or history. Though it is prohibited, overnight campers have been known to make use of the beach, building fires along its edge. Occasional parties also occur. Locals mainly use the shoreline to gain access to the lake for waterfowl hunting in the fall or just to get onto Cougar Bay with their canoes or kayaks. It is one of Lake Coeur d'Alene's more natural and secluded public areas.

The BLM sign at the former Healy property. *Author's collection.*

CHAPTER 5

OPPOSITION DOUBLES DOWN

Find a way to get in the way.
—*John Lewis*

TENACIOUS RESISTANCE

Immediately after the meeting in Scott Reed's office in March 1993, some former members of the Friends of Cougar Bay formed a new nonprofit citizens' group called Rural Kootenai Organization (RKO) to champion Cougar Bay's further preservation. As previously explained, over the winter of 1993, McCormack Properties acquired an additional 118 acres from the Earl Johnson family southwest of the Healy land. McCormack's development plan, named the Ridge at Cougar Bay, called for a ninety-two-home subdivision on the hillside.

McCormack first proposed drilling a water well on-site. In response, opponents presented evidence to the county that groundwater was in short supply south of the Spokane River. This led to the county commissioners requiring McCormack to get water off-site. As a result, he proposed running a water line from Central Pre-Mix's property (now the Riverstone Development) under the Spokane River and over Blackwell Hill to the subdivision. In addition, he wanted to construct an on-site wastewater treatment system. This was denied. He later built a community septic system and drain field.

McCormack pledged he would designate the eighty acres of submerged land purchased from the Healy family as a wildlife sanctuary (gift) if county officials approved his proposed ninety-two-home upland subdivision. He believed, as did others living next to the bay, that he owned the submerged land in front of the shoreline since he was being taxed a small amount for it by the county. Indeed, the county does tax some lakeshore property owners' submerged land using the "Flood Land" pricing system. As a result, the submerged land is valued at ten dollars per acre. Most parcels are charged around ten to twenty cents in taxes per year. It turned out that even though private property owners paid minimal taxes on submerged land, they did not have the right to determine its use. The State of Idaho has the only jurisdiction, as determined by a December 1999 Idaho Supreme Court decision.[11]

This sanctuary "gift" was questioned by RKO because it suggested secret dealings between McCormack and the county. Because of these proposals, RKO became an even more relentless watchdog. The group did not want to see the hillside sacrificed to save the shoreline. Without fully realizing it, RKO's persistence in slowing the Ridge development afforded time for other events to occur. The long battle to curb the development would eventually lead to Cougar Bay's preservation.

THE RIDGE AT COUGAR BAY

RKO's skepticism about McCormack Properties' motives was clarified in an RKO news brief written in 1995, titled "The Cougar Bay Illusion or Where Is that Public Wildlife Sanctuary?" The news brief was cleverly written in a theatrical play format with a setting, cast of characters and three-act plot. The newsletter described how the funds for the Healy property were manipulated to look like the actual Healy 11.64-acre shoreline property was worth more because it included some 80 acres of submerged land. In fact, the State of Idaho owned the submerged lands, as acknowledged by McCormack Properties' March 10, 1994 quitclaim deed.

A few weeks after the 1995 newsletter came out, the Kootenai County Planning and Zoning Commission and later the county commissioners were asked at public hearings who really owned Cougar Bay's submerged land and whether it could be "gifted." The county chose not to investigate ownership and approved McCormack's Ridge project. This triggered RKO to file a lawsuit asking a state district judge to overrule the county's decision.

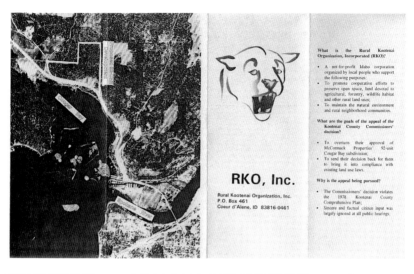

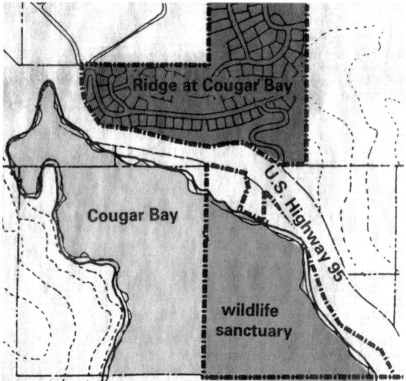

Top: Rural Kootenai Organization newsletter. *Author's collection.*

Bottom: Cougar Bay Ridge map. *Courtesy of the* Spokesman Review.

Rural Kootenai Organization Raises the Bar

Anticipating the lawsuit's cost, RKO quickly started raising funds for legal appeals and fees. It hired two local environmental attorneys, Charles Sheroke and Marc McGregor, to challenge the commissioners' approval. RKO held fundraisers including pancake feeds, bake sales, yard sales, art auctions, dances at the Mica Grange Hall and even a chuck wagon dinner. By 1996, RKO had collected more than $24,000 in donations and attracted a remarkable array of community support. In addition, the attorneys charged half their normal fees. Donations poured in to oppose the Ridge, including an $8,500 grant from the Bullitt Foundation. The Idaho Conservation League worked as a partner on the Bullitt grant by assisting with any financial obligations. One anonymous donor pitched in $20,000.

During the fundraising, the district judge decided in favor of the county's decision to approve McCormack's subdivision as presented. In response, RKO appealed the ruling to the Idaho Supreme Court. In 1999, the court overturned the district court decision and remanded the county's approval back to the county commissioners for reconsideration. It determined that the State of Idaho had jurisdiction over land beneath state waters. Subsequently, the county commissioners approved McCormack's subdivision proposal without the wildlife sanctuary.

In a conversation with a former RKO member, I realized how difficult it is for outsiders to comprehend the financial and emotional toll of this fight. She remembered when the $20,000 check arrived in RKO's post office box. She recalled breaking down and weeping in the post office. An elderly gentleman asked her if she needed assistance. She replied, "No, thank you. I was just given a miracle."

This same RKO member kept all the boxes of paperwork dealing with the Cougar Bay campaign. They included RKO's articles, newsletters and legal papers and the Friends' efforts. She held on to them for over a decade. But one day, she called another RKO member and asked him to come and pick up the boxes or she would take them to the dump. He picked them up. These boxes contained a treasure-trove of information on this complex struggle. Gertie Hanson, Wes's deceased wife, had saved every bit of information from the battle. This book sprang from that material.

It is exhausting to be an activist, even for a short-lived project. But this battle went on for over a decade. Environmental activists can fall victim to their own martyrdom. To avoid this, RKO adopted a local resolve that was sensitive to nature and openly defended it. Its underlying goal was Cougar

Bay's preservation. To do this, it steadily engaged in the hearing and legal processes. The group's pugnacious spirit was extraordinary.

RKO was unwavering in its effort to postpone McCormack's 118-acre development. From 1993 to 2001, RKO delayed the Ridge development. Unwittingly, RKO kept Cougar Bay's future in the limelight. The community and The Nature Conservancy realized its worth and quietly supported the preservation effort.

THE NATURE CONSERVANCY STEPS UP AGAIN

During the 1990s, The Nature Conservancy stepped up its effort to save Cougar Bay from development. In June 1997, after serving earlier as an intermediary for the BLM to buy the Healy north shore property, The Nature Conservancy signed an option with Crown Pacific Lumber Company to buy two parcels of land on the bay. It totaled 88.51 acres on Cougar Bay's south shore. The property encompassed 1,300 feet of undeveloped shoreline.

This was TNC's first permanent acquisition in Kootenai County. The Nature Conservancy raised $245,000 to buy the property, about $75,000 below the assessed fair market value. Larry Isenberg, Crown Pacific's timber and land manager at the time, said the company agreed to sell the property at a reduced price to give TNC a head start in raising funds to make the project (a nature preserve) successful. This was a win-win agreement between Crown Pacific and The Conservancy. Crown Pacific kept its adjoining tree farm property above Cougar Bay next to the 88.51 acres. Isenberg stated that preserving a quality environment and supporting forest product jobs were compatible. It was Crown Pacific's generosity that enabled The Nature Conservancy to continue its work by purchasing land for the Cougar Bay Nature Preserve.

Cougar Bay welcome sign. *Author's collection.*

The Ridge Changes Hands, 2000–2002

In 2000, McCormack defaulted on land payments owed on the proposed ninety-two-home upland subdivision, the Ridge at Cougar Bay. Some of McCormack's financial problems stemmed from the legal fees he faced from RKO's persistent lawsuits and appeals, and some of his problems were caused by his other real estate investments and developments. A sheriff's sale was held in July 2000. The land was purchased back by the Earl Johnson family, though McCormack was given one year to redeem the property before it legally went back to the Johnsons. Starting in July 2001 (the one-year sheriff's sale deadline), the Johnson family granted McCormack Properties a series of extensions as McCormack began negotiating a settlement with Rural Kootenai Organization. McCormack was exhausted and losing money.

In the fall of 2001, McCormack, RKO and the county negotiated an agreement to create a thirty-three-acre conservation easement next to the Ridge at Cougar Bay in exchange for platting a smaller seventy-seven-lot subdivision. The parties then enlisted the Inland Northwest Land Trust (now called the Inland Northwest Land Conservancy) to accept and monitor the conservation easement. In 2002, McCormack Properties sold the Ridge property to developer Bill Radobanko. Radobanko honored the agreement and on December 30, 2003, executed the conservation agreement, ensuring permanent protection of the thirty-three acres. The Conservancy walks the property every year to make sure it remains undeveloped with its conservation values intact. No houses occupy the forested hillside fronting the highway and facing Cougar Bay, where at least a dozen houses might have been constructed, absent the original agreement and permanent protection.

Why a Conservation Easement?

Many people ask what a conservation easement is. A conservation easement establishes a landowner's vision and memorializes a commitment to the conservation of a property. The easement protects private lands in perpetuity from land-use development that could destroy a property's agricultural, wildlife, biological or scenic values.[12] According to Idaho Code, conservation easements must accomplish at least one of the following purposes: "retaining or protecting natural, scenic, or open-space values of real property, assuring its availability for agricultural, forest, recreational, or open-space use, protecting natural resources, maintaining or enhancing air or water quality, or preserving the historical, architectural, archaeological, or cultural aspects of real property."[13]

A conservation easement is a legal agreement that is voluntarily negotiated between a property owner and a qualified land trust or government agency. When signed, the agreement is recorded at a courthouse. Every conservation easement is unique. Some allow public access, while others do not. In north Idaho and eastern Washington, the Inland Northwest Land Conservancy is the qualified conservation organization that facilitates conservation easements.[14]

CHAPTER 6

PRESERVING THE REST
OF COUGAR BAY

Every aspect of our lives is, in a sense,
a vote for the kind of world we want to live in.
—Frances Moore Lappé

JOHN POINTNER: DELTA CONTROL, DYNAMITE, HEART OF THE ENVIRONMENT

One piece of privately owned Cougar Bay land and submerged marsh was still needed to complete the preservation of Cougar Bay. John C. Pointner owned 160 acres at the southwestern end of Cougar Bay. Pointner grew up in Coeur d'Alene, where his father owned a machine shop. John received a bachelor's degree in mechanical engineering from the University of Idaho in 1947 and then moved back to Coeur d'Alene and worked as a machinist, building his shop where the southernmost dock is located on Cougar Bay at 3730 South Highway 95. This is where a large log home and outbuilding are now located. The Craftsman log home was formerly used as the Casco Bay summer residence of the Hagadone family, who own the *Coeur d'Alene Press*. The log home was purchased by Rocky and Mary Watson, who saved the historic structure from demolition. The caveat was that the Watsons had to move the home from Casco Bay to their lakefront property (formerly John Pointner's shop locale) at Cougar Bay. It was barged around the point in 2008 to the scenic western shoreline of Cougar Bay. The log home was sold in 2018 and has become an owner-occupied bed-and-breakfast appropriately named the Cougar Bay Lodge.

Most locals knew Pointner as an eccentric, determined man who thought of himself as Cougar Bay's self-appointed defender. In the early 1980s, over a two-year period, he and his friend Greg Nearpass, a self-described dynamite expert, placed dynamite sticks throughout Cougar Bay, presumably to loosen sediment and make canals. In doing so, Pointner hoped to develop what he called a "delta control" system, a hodgepodge of dredged canals and settlement basins designed to trap sediment flowing into Cougar Bay from Cougar Creek. Using a hydraulic dredger, Pointner dug his preliminary ditch three feet deep, six feet wide and four thousand feet long as well as a fifteen-foot-deep settling basin near his buildings. Next, he excavated a settling basin along the south hillside that was six hundred feet long, one hundred feet wide and ten feet deep. He then bulldozed one thousand feet along the bay's southern hillside edge. Pointner's numerous canals are still evident in the bay and used by paddlers. Even now, you can see his large rusted Allis-Chalmers bulldozer parked along Cougar Bay's south shoreline trail. Children love to climb on the monstrous machine.

John worked most days in his Cougar Bay machine shop, making all kinds of gadgets and fixing people's machines. One of the most unusual machines he designed and built was a "swamp buggy," an oversized motorized contraption with gigantic cleated steel wheels. He used it to get around the marshy bay. Lore has it that he laid planks in the marsh and drove on them with his equipment. You can drive by the swamp buggy on West Riverview Drive near Post Falls. How it got there is unknown.

Pointner's single-minded focus was revealed in a paid advertisement in the *Coeur d'Alene Press*, dated September 16, 1992. Pointner wrote his story titled "Obituary of Cougar Bay." It began, "Cougar Bay Marsh, heart of the environment, is owned by John Pointner. It is healthy because I have taken care of it. Without the marsh, environmentally speaking, the area would be like a picture frame without the picture. Hillsides surrounding a stinking cesspool mud flat would have existed for twenty years if I had not prevented it." It appeared that Pointner was agitated by the recently enacted regulations against dredging and excavating on all of Lake Coeur d'Alene. New policies required transporting all material excavated below the lake's ordinary high-water level to remote higher ground. The lake was greatly contaminated from mining tailings from a century of gold and silver mining in the Silver Valley. Much of the waste material contained toxic or environmentally hazardous substances such as cadmium, lead and zinc. This material was directly discharged or washed into the South Fork of the Coeur d'Alene River and its tributaries that flowed into Lake Coeur d'Alene.[15] Nevertheless,

Cougar Bay might not be as contaminated as the main lake. Some pollutants were neutralized by Cougar Bay's soils, dense vegetation and slow-moving water. Wetland soils often can neutralize some contaminants.[16]

Pointner's half-page advertisement proclaimed that he alone had saved Cougar Bay and clearly revealed his self-anointment as Cougar Bay's savior. In his opinion, if the county didn't complete the delta control protection of Cougar Bay, "no vegetation or wildlife will be left alive and only a barren stinking mud flat cesspool will remain." He also asked that the Cougar Gulch watershed property owners and McCormack's proposed subdivision be taxed to fund his cleanup of the marsh. He continued, saying that he was seventy-three years old and did not have the money or strength to carry on, but he would advise how the marsh could be saved. He ended the paid advertisement with saying that Cougar Bay's "only hope for continued environmental viability is to protect the marsh as a well-cared for Aquatic Wildlife Park with no encroachment by man in the wetland other than to enhance and protect it. I have done my job for thirty years. I know how to do it. Now let someone else do it for the next hundred years." The full advertisement can be seen in Appendix C.

Despite Pointner's bristly character, his hopes have come to pass. Cougar Bay is now a nature preserve. The Bureau of Land Management is also digging canals throughout the shallowest part of the bay to remove invasive grasses and restore Cougar Creek's natural flow.

During the rest of the 1990s, Pointner tried to sell the land. He approached The Nature Conservancy. It declined. Then he tempted Gonzaga University with an idea that it could create a biology field station where students could conduct research studies. The deal collapsed when Coeur d'Alene businessman Duane Hagadone refused to give the university an easement through his adjacent property. Pointner bargained with the University of Idaho as well. It, too, declined.

Simultaneously, the BLM and the county were also negotiating with Pointner. Scott Forsell, former BLM acquisitions manager, worked with John during this time. Forsell stated at some point that John had the property appraised but when it came back at $1.1 million, he promptly fired the appraiser. He said it was worth at least $3 million. Part of the issue on selling his land was that Duane Hagadone owned property south of Pointner's property. Some of it intruded into Pointner's land beside the bay. Hagadone at the time said no to Pointner's request to widen the easement from ten to fifteen feet for a public road. Pointner held a grudge against Hagadone over this for the rest of his life. One of the county employees who worked with

Forsell had John's ear and felt she had some influence with him. She kept the negotiations going. However, every time the BLM talked to him, John would change the rules, such as saying, "Now I want mineral rights" or "I've got other people interested in buying the land for far more money." It was a most frustrating ordeal. BLM finally told him enough was enough; the game was over. John replied, "But I'm having so much fun." It seems the Allis-Chalmers bulldozer that sits along the shoreline trail is an apt symbol of John Pointner's way of thinking. BLM asked him if he would sell it so it could move the beast. He kept saying he knew people who were "extremely interested in it." They were not.[17] The bulldozer will sit next to Cougar Bay's shoreline indefinitely.

Finally, in April 2003 at the age of eighty-four, after suffering a series of strokes over the years, Pointner struck an unusual deal with the U.S. Bureau of Land Management and Kootenai County: 155 of his 160 acres would become public land, intended for wildlife and wetland preservation and public recreation. Pointner retained 5 acres where the Coeur d'Alene Machine and Repair Works sat next to the bay. The BLM was concerned with the machine shop's possible contamination and declined to buy it.

The sale used an inventive contract, with the BLM and Kootenai County paying Pointner $5,000 a month until he died. The BLM would pay $3,500

The view from Pointner's shop. *Courtesy of the* Spokesman Review.

a month, while the county picked up the remaining $1,500. Pointner agreed to forgive the debt after his death. Part of the agreement was that the sanctuary be named the John C. Pointner Memorial Wildlife Sanctuary and that his ashes be spread across the bay. At that time, he bought a three-foot stone memorial that read, "Dead People and Live Animals Permitted." It is placed at an undisclosed location on the land surrounding Cougar Bay. The agreement was that the county would manage the water and marshland while the BLM would oversee the upland ground and timber. John Pointner died twenty-five months later on Memorial Day, May 30, 2005. Because of this agreement, most of Cougar Bay would be saved from development.

CHAPTER 7

THE COUGAR BAY NATURE PRESERVE
TODAY AND TOMORROW

In wildness is the preservation of the world.
—*Henry David Thoreau*

To complete the jigsaw puzzle that makes up the Cougar Bay Nature Preserve, two acres adjacent to the Crown Pacific Timber Company land were gifted by the Earl Johnson family to The Nature Conservancy in June 2005. The bay had finally been securely saved from development. At this point, Duane Hagadone generously allowed the proposed BLM trail to cross his property.

The 1.2-mile John C. Pointner Memorial Wildlife Sanctuary section of the trail meanders along Cougar Bay's southern shoreline. The trail lies in the 155-acre parcel managed by the BLM. The BLM's later acquisition of 88.51 acres from The Nature Conservancy in 2021 adds 1 mile to the trail system. The road leading to the preserve's parking lot is named after the McAvoy family, who once owned the land above Cougar Creek. When Herb McAvoy died, Crown Pacific bought his 177.2-acre property in the 1990s, later selling part of it to The Nature Conservancy.

Public feedback regarding options for the trail occurred in 2012 and 2013. The BLM then conducted an environmental assessment and flagged the trail in. Due to limited staff and the BLM's planning cycle, getting the trail constructed took some time. The actual trail construction was primarily done by the U.S. Forest Service fire hotshot crew in the spring of 2014. The crew did most of the heavy lifting, as some of the area is rocky and unstable.

Josh Kirby and his dad at the finished lookout platform. *Bureau of Land Management.*

Post Falls Boy Scout Troup 209 constructing the viewing platform at Cougar Bay. *Bureau of Land Management.*

After this, the BLM held a National Trails Day event, and volunteers—including teenagers from the Anchor House, a residential treatment center for boys—helped finish the trail.

The reward for reaching the highest point of the trail is an overlook that offers not only a resting point but also spectacular views of Lake Coeur d'Alene. The viewing platform was constructed in the summer of 2014 by Post Falls Boy Scout Troop 209. The effort was led by Eagle Scout Josh Kirby. Through a partnership with the Boy Scouts, the BLM procured the platform materials, and the Scouts provided the labor.

As you hike on the 2.2-mile trail, you will pass by a bench installed by The Nature Conservancy that sits under a large cottonwood tree. Hikers can rest and enjoy the view of a wild marsh teeming with waterfowl and other birds. The bench features a plaque with a notable quotation from anthropologist Margaret Mead: "Never doubt that a small group of thoughtful, committed citizens can change the world. Indeed, it is the only thing that ever has." Fittingly, this is exactly what happened to preserve Cougar Bay. Near the cottonwood tree, the Coeur d'Alene Audubon Society installed several birdhouses dedicated to local wildlife supporters. Along the trail, you will see trail markers offering wildlife, plant and wetland information. These were donated by the Coeur d'Alene and Spokane Audubon societies and private sponsors. The nature preserve also provides a picturesque entryway into the city of Coeur d'Alene. If you are looking northeast from the bay, the city can be seen in the background, making for a scenic view, especially at night.

BLM ACQUIRES THE COUGAR BAY NATURE PRESERVE, 2021

In 2021, the Bureau of Land Management purchased the Cougar Bay Nature Preserve (88.51 acres) from The Nature Conservancy. The BLM utilized $1.6 million from the Land and Water Conservation Fund (LWCF) to complete the transaction. The purchase directly aligned with the Biden administration's America the Beautiful initiative by conserving, connecting and working to restore public lands. According to Robyn Miller, deputy director of The Nature Conservancy in Idaho, "This next step in our partnership with the BLM ensures sensitive lakefront wildlife habitat will remain undeveloped while continuing to offer recreational opportunities for the community."

With the acquisition, the Cougar Bay Nature Preserve expanded to total 243.51 acres.

RESTORATION EFFORTS

Cougar Creek and associated wetlands at Cougar Bay have historically been channelized and altered for agricultural purposes. This reduced their ecological functions and habitat values. At one point, Cougar Creek was diverted by a man-made ditch, most likely dug by a farmer. A culvert was also put in by the Idaho Transportation Department when new Highway 95 was constructed near the bay. These changes along with hay farming and upstream development caused the bay to fill with invasive grasses that plugged water flow.[18]

The BLM has undertaken a three-year wetland restoration project in partnership with Ducks Unlimited. The Cougar Bay Wetlands Enhancement project will remove invasive reed canary grass that has negatively impacted water dispersal. Working together, they have dug a main channel from the Cougar Creek bridge to Cougar Bay to help disseminate water flow.

Raised mounded areas and ponds were constructed during channel excavation to facilitate diversity in habitat, vegetation and water depth. The new channels were also designed to allow frequent overflow of water into

Cougar Bay channel work by BLM. *Author's collection.*

the wetlands. The invasive reed canary grass was treated with herbicides as a temporary suppression to allow newly seeded native grasses to take hold. The Bureau of Land Management states that the Cougar Bay wetlands restoration will enhance habitat for waterfowl and fish, improve water quality in Cougar Creek and Coeur d'Alene Lake and restore native riparian vegetation along a properly functioning wetland channel.[19]

Ducks Unlimited (DU), a 501(c) nonprofit organization, partners with a wide range of corporations, governments, non-governmental organizations and landowners to restore degraded wetlands. In partnership with the Bureau of Land Management, DU's conservation plan for Cougar Bay will diversify waterfowl and other wildlife habitats. The project is being funding through a $282,000 grant from the Restoration Partnership, a group of federal, state and tribal entities spearheading natural resource restoration in the Coeur d'Alene Basin.

CHAPTER 8

THREATS TO COUGAR BAY

Plans to protect air and water, wilderness and wildlife
are in fact plans to protect man.
—*Stewart Udall, secretary of interior (1961–69)*

One of the first threats to Cougar Bay's wetlands came about in the summer of 1983. Construction of the "new" U.S. 95 going north and south of Coeur d'Alene was in full swing. The "old" U.S. 95 had meandered around the bay and marshland through Cougar Gulch. The Idaho Transportation Department (ITD) built the new four-lane highway directly through the marshy portion of Cougar Bay. A swath across the length of the wetland from the northeast shore to the southwest shore was filled to build the new highway. While the roadway was being constructed, ITD dumped excess fill dirt (called the McAvoy fill) near the northeast shore without the necessary U.S. Army Corps of Engineers 404 permit. This permit is required by the Clean Water Act, which is a broad-based law covering water pollution control. ITD proposed mitigating the fill in 1986. It planned to alter the McAvoy fill to match the existing wetland.[20] This plan, named the Cougar Bay Wetlands Project, avoided the costly removal of the fill. In the meantime, the Idaho Fish and Game Non-Game Advisory Committee was alerted about the plan.

A spokesperson for the Idaho Department of Fish and Game, Region 1 Non-Game Advisory Committee, spoke at an ITD public hearing in 1987. The purpose of the hearing was to allow testimony on the Cougar Bay

Wetlands Project. The committee was concerned about the damage caused by the McAvoy fill. The committee had four recommendations: there would be no shooting or hunting allowed; a parking area would be provided so the public wouldn't be exposed to traffic hazards; the design would allow public access and viewing in such a way that it would not be detrimental to wildlife; and finally, a qualified person with knowledge of wildlife would be included in the planning.

The committee stressed that historically, the Cougar Bay meadows have provided a stopover for migrating waterfowl as well as habitat for a wide range of birds and animals. They also emphasized Cougar Bay's unique value to the community, offering an easily accessible observation place for the public to enjoy. Ultimately, though, the committee recommended removal of the fill and restoration of the 3.2 acres. After reviewing the mitigation plan, the U.S. Corps of Engineers forced ITD to remove the 3.2 acres of fill and take it to a safe and suitable area.

Some mitigation was done after the removal of the fill; however, wetlands are fragile. The mitigation of damaged wetlands has a very poor record because technology cannot replicate nature, particularly of forested or peated wetlands. Time has helped with the restoration of the damage at Cougar Bay, but the 3.2 acres will never be the same.

What is most interesting is the foresight of the Non-Game Advisory Committee's recommendations. The fill dirt was removed. As time passed, the parking lot was constructed and trails and a viewing platform were created. The wetlands were left to thrive except for some restoration projects.

More Threats

Longtime Cougar Bay resident and tugboat operator Ed Haglund said one of the biggest environmental threats to Cougar Bay is invasive plant species. They include milfoil, pond leaf and yellow flag iris, which can take over large areas of the bay's water. The bay's invasive reed canary grass has caused a dam of sorts, keeping water dispersal to a minimum and closing off the channels. These channels carry water into and around the bay. The channels are used by wading birds and waterfowl, as well as painted turtles and frogs. Moose like to forage in these more open areas. Haglund stated that the good news is freshwater celery and water sponges are thriving in the bay, which means the water quality is still good.

Moose in Cougar Bay. *Courtesy Cara Anthony at Cougar Bay Lodge.*

A different and ongoing pressure to Cougar Bay is noncompliance with the rules and regulations regarding activities on Lake Coeur d'Alene, specifically that of seasonal and year-round dock storage in Cougar Bay. Though Lake Coeur d'Alene has a history of industrial use, including tugboats and sawmills, times have changed. As mentioned before, mill logs were stored in Cougar Bay. Seasonally stored boat docks have replaced them. In 2023, the north end of the bay near the marina was still being used for dock storage. North Idaho Maritime and its predecessors have been using this part of the bay for decades as a temporary holding yard and repair station for wayward docks. North Idaho Maritime finally applied for an Idaho Department of Lands encroachment permit in 2020 for the use of ten acres of Cougar Bay's surface waters. Based on substantial evidence in the record and conclusions of law, the encroachment permit was initially denied by the Idaho Department of Lands (IDL). Maritime's permit application proposed keeping the docks in a corral and creating a dock repair area. The longtime use of Cougar Bay as a salvage yard had reached a tipping point. Community members believed the bay should not be degraded any longer by any industrial operation. The denied permit has since been reversed. North Idaho Maritime was given a lease beginning on January 1, 2021, with an expiration date of December 31, 2030, at $5,000 per year.[21]

Dock storage on Cougar Bay. *Courtesy Rod Stach.*

William Stach, a Cougar Bay resident for over fifty years, lives directly across from Maritime's dock area. He said the Cougar Bay Water Association is concerned about Maritime's continued use of Cougar Bay, its impact on the lake's beauty, and the safety of recreational users. He believes the ongoing storage and repair station at the north end of Cougar Bay threatens the ecological and aesthetic character of the bay. The broken-down docks are barely floating and simply left like garbage in the bay. Congestion is another issue. The entrance to Cougar Bay where it meets Lake Coeur d'Alene has a marina on its north side. The BLM also has boat ramps next to the marina. If paddlers don't put in at the bay itself, they must use the BLM docks and paddle through the congested Hagadone marina to get to the bay. Collisions have happened in this area. It's just a matter of time before there is a serious accident. However, Kootenai County designated Cougar Bay itself as a no-wake zone. This has kept Cougar Bay's Nature Preserve quiet and natural. Canoeists and kayakers paddle through the wetland without worry of motorized watercraft.

Another concern is that Murphy Marine Construction Company already stores about 150 docks in Cougar Bay each winter. The company subleases the storage site from North Idaho Maritime. Murphy's company collects the docks in mid-October and stores them in the sheltered bay until May. Murphy Marine said that storing the docks keeps them from breaking free in high water and becoming a navigational hazard. Nevertheless, the dock storage creates its own hazard. Boats get stuck in the corral formed by chained logs. One homeowner said on summer nights he has had to take his boat out and guide trapped watercraft out of the corral with his flashlight.

Inside one of the islands of debris owned by Murphy Marine sits a large crumbling water slide/jungle gym of what was once called Hooligan Island, an attempted—now defunct—floating entertainment business that has been in the bay since 2018. The water attraction showed up in 2017 just off the city beach. The idea was to charge people to let them use the island of nonstop fun. City leaders said the owners of Hooligan Island did not have permission to do that. The island appeared again a month later near North Idaho College, as the owners continued to work toward obtaining a business license. But they were using a dock owned by North Idaho College to conduct business without permission. The school kicked them out. A couple of months later, things seemed to be going well for the Hooligan crew. They moved farther offshore. A few weeks later, the owners posted on Facebook that the six-hundred-square-foot island was for sale. Since then, it has been kept among the derelict docks and boats in the middle of Cougar Bay. The Hooligan Island Facebook page is dormant.

Idaho Department of Lands stated it was working with North Idaho Maritime to clean up its many derelict docks cluttering the bay. Some of the junk docks have been cleaned out. The StanCraft company bought out North Idaho Maritime in late 2022. StanCraft states it is proud of its local involvement. It has built and maintained numerous facilities for public entities on local, state and federal levels. It has restored and protected miles of shoreline, removed hazardous pilings and debris from state waterways and removed tons of contaminated soils from local lakes and rivers. It has also played a role in placing gravel bedding to support fish habitats and has installed nesting platforms for birds. It remains to be seen if StanCraft will be a good steward of Cougar Bay.

Other than these genuine threats, Cougar Bay is thriving as a nature preserve. The Cougar Bay Nature Preserve provides protection to its wetland fringe. Over 150 bird species have been sighted and recorded in and around Cougar Bay's wetlands (see Appendix F). The Nature Conservancy's 88-acre site plus the adjacent 155-acre John C. Pointner Memorial Sanctuary provides habitat for a wide range of wildlife. The nature preserve protects an

Hooligan Island. *Author's collection.*

undisturbed wetland fringe for Lake Coeur d'Alene, which serves as a nursery area for fish and waterfowl. These riparian areas where habitats intersect are called "edges." The greater number of landscape elements and vegetation complexity results in greater density and biodiversity. This phenomenon is called the "edge effect." For example, you will always find a greater number of bird species along the land-water edges. The wetlands at Cougar Bay also sustain important ecological functions by trapping sediment that might otherwise reach the lake.

Locals and travelers wander the 2.2 miles of trails that encircle the preserve year-round. While highway sounds are inescapable on the trails, the area is one of the few public access areas left on Lake Coeur d'Alene. It and the BLM's 11-acre north shore parcel are maintained as primitive wildlife areas. No restrooms, drinking water or trash pickup are provided.

CHAPTER 9

THE LEGACY OF COUGAR BAY

Out, away to the world with hope.
—*William Kittredge,* Hole in the Sky

The Cougar Bay Nature Preserve could have easily been cut up into housing lots with docks jutting into one of the most beautiful lakes in the world. The preserve exists because determined activists intervened, landowners cooperated and both private groups and public agencies became involved in acquiring public ownership. One could also say that Cougar Bay's preservation came about in sometimes mysterious ways, through synchronicities and events we call coincidences or even miracles. This hard-won nature preserve is a rare phenomenon in a county where private development is a priority. As the late Scott Reed, author of *The Treasure Called Tubbs Hill*, stated, "Public ownership is the surest way to preserve and protect property."

Public lands such as the Cougar Bay Nature Preserve are undeniably good for our community. The Preserve ensures that this special outdoor place is held in trust for future generations. It is a diverse wetland that is on the mend thanks to the Cougar Bay Wetlands Enhancement project and Ducks Unlimited.

Whether they are local, federal or regional, public lands provide ecological, social, economic, lifestyle and health benefits. For example, Cougar Bay provides wildlife habitats and clean water in addition to recreational hiking, boating and fishing. It also promotes tourism; families benefit from memorable experiences, and photographers can take wildlife pictures to their heart's content.

When I hike the Cougar Bay Nature Preserve trail, I am reminded that life is most abundant in nature. The forest and waters calm my ever-busy mind. I become open to listening and observing the natural landscape. Violet green swallows swoop and sing their *chee-chee-chee* song while my eyes may linger on a long-neck western grebe diving for fish. This wetland is filled with a natural world that we humans cannot fully imagine. I usually see scat from deer and bear signifying I am in their world. I stop in my tracks to listen to the haunting great horned owl's call, *hoo-hoo-oo, hoo hoo*, enchanted by its very nature. An abandoned apple orchard above the hiking trail feeds bears and even hikers in the fall. Here is a place where people and nature intersect, where both are free to thrive. And isn't this Cougar Bay's essential gift? The Cougar Bay Nature Preserve is a legacy that belongs to us all.

CHAPTER 10

A COLLECTION OF LOCAL STORIES ON LIFE AT COUGAR BAY

The clearest way into the Universe is through a forest wilderness.
—*John Muir*

MY FIRST OSPREY

I was paddling across Cougar Bay in my canoe when I saw a bird plunge into the water. At first, I thought it was an eagle. Then it rose in a commotion of flapping wings and water, carrying a fish that weighed it down. I wondered if the bird's wet wings would lift it and its meal. Gradually, the bird rose and landed on a nest, where it killed the fish and with its hooked beak tore morsels for its young. I described what I had seen to a friend, telling him it must have been an eagle. He looked at me and told me it was probably an osprey.

BLUE HERONS IN COUGAR BAY'S WETLAND

Like most birds, great blue herons shy away from humans. The nearer we come, the farther they move off until finally they betray their hiding places by flapping their slate gray wings. They glide above reed tops and wheel to gain altitude. In flight, their long necks are tucked, and stilt-thin legs line up with tails. Odd as it sounds, they land in pine trees on Cougar Bay's southern shore, where little will disturb them. They stare down from limbs and, when we leave, glide to the reeds again.

FISH STORY

I was kayaking on Cougar Bay with my daughter. She was four years old. I usually fly-fish, but the bay is shallow and filled with weeds, especially where the lake turns into wetland. That evening, I cast plugs near reeds. Suddenly, my rod tip tugged down and the fish, whatever it was, started pulling us around the bay. This was all right for a while. I figured the fish would wear out soon and I would reel it in, net it and go home. But my daughter pointed at the zigging line. It dawned on me this could go on indefinitely. So I finally cut the line. Later, someone told me Cougar Bay contained trophy-size pike.

LEAVING U.S. 95 PADDLING SOUTH

If you pull off U.S. 95 on the north shore of Cougar Bay, don't get hit by oncoming traffic. You park in a wide gravel strip that fronts the Bureau of Land Management's property. The eleven acres or so that face Cougar Bay were saved from development in the 1990s. With traffic whizzing by, you take off your kayak or canoe and carry it down a well-worn curving path to the edge of the bay. The shore is usually clogged by floating logs. There is no formal launching place, so you wade in carefully. It's so easy to tip over. In a few strokes, the roar of the highway fades, and you cut through smooth water. Water drips from paddle blades. Looking down, you see rising vegetation. Minutes later, you have crossed the bay and rest in slack water filled by reflections of green trees. U.S. 95 is so far away, though occasionally you hear a truck downshift and see black diesel belch rising into the sky.

GETTING AWAY

I run my dogs on the trails above The Nature Conservancy's Cougar Bay Preserve. The first thing they do is wade into the marsh and slurp water. That's happiness to them. They trot ahead and sniff. The younger dog follows his curiosity, chasing sounds he hears, movements and smells, until they bore him or fade away and he returns to the trail. The older dog, who used to meander, now follows me. We walk the trails made by boys from Anchor House up switchbacks and over basalt outcrops. The dogs see this as an adventure. For me, it is a chance to get out of the house and see nature close at hand, just minutes away.

The Bench

I like to go out to Cougar Bay and walk over the bridge that crosses Cougar Creek. The overgrown road bends left, following the dips and rises of the shore. I hear blackbirds' hoarse calls and watch as swallows dive and linger in flight. There is a bench ahead dedicated to conservationist Mannie Scherr. The Nature Conservancy placed it there to honor him. A small plaque reads, "Never doubt that a small group of thoughtful citizens can change the world. Indeed, it's the only thing that ever has." When I sit on that bench, I am confident Cougar Bay will be preserved as a wild and natural public place.

Quiet Flotilla

The other night, I paddled across Cougar Bay in a kayak. We launched into the lake from the Bureau of Land Management recreation site at Blackwell Island. The group I was with negotiated the compact channel through the Blackwell Island Marina and came out into calm, cool water. I hadn't paddled a kayak before and had only driven by Cougar Bay. That night, as our group went around log pilings, nesting osprey screamed at us and went back to tending their fledglings.

Old U.S. 95

Going south, U.S. 95 used to follow the contours of Cougar Bay and the Meadowbrook marsh, climbing Mica Hill in a series of curving switchbacks. I used to drive my VW Bug late at night to Mica Flats to pick up jugs of fresh milk. The night sky above Mica Flats glistened with stars. There wasn't a lot of traffic. Returning to Coeur d'Alene, I watched town lights replace stars. It was dark at the bottom of the Mica grade. The shoreline was undeveloped, as it is today. Cougar Bay was so close to the hubbub of Coeur d'Alene yet could have been many miles away. I wondered then about its future.

Two Eagles

Most people watch eagles perching on snags or skimming low to snatch a dead kokanee at Wolf Lodge Bay, on Lake Coeur d'Alene's southeast side.

I've done that, too. But last year, I paddled to the south side of Cougar Bay and ended up floating below an overhanging Ponderosa pine. Two eagles sat on limbs. One had a white head; the other was mottled gray and brown. They studied me and must have thought I was harmless. Of course, I didn't have a camera or binoculars with me. Such moments last in memory long after treasured photographs are lost. I watched them cock their heads as I bobbed past.

John Pointner and the BLM

John Pointner owned 160 acres around and under Cougar Bay. He ran a machine shop on its western shore. He had big plans for Cougar Bay. One of them was to dredge channels to catch silt flushed down from Cougar Creek. A lawsuit stopped this when it was partly done. Eventually, John sold his land to the Bureau of Land Management. That's why the public owns Cougar Bay's south shore. Sometime soon hiking trails will cross it, bringing people close to nature and allowing them to overlook Cougar Bay's calm water.

When I Was a Little Girl

When I was a little girl, I liked to explore spots beyond where the lawn ended. I preferred wet places like lake shores and swamps. I helped my brothers build forts and liked to walk around imagining other worlds. I have this same yearning when I walk around Cougar Bay. This is the place, other than Tubbs Hill, where children can explore the world and release their imaginations. I hope we are smart enough to leave Cougar Bay intact for my grandchildren and yours.

Growing Up

In the 1940s and '50s, Cougar Bay was a wild and wondrous place for a young boy. We used to call it the Meadows. There was one house along the shore where a boat was kept on its dock. I obtained permission to use the boat often. The water and shore were crawling with wildlife, like bullfrogs, turtles, songbirds and blue herons. There weren't as many ducks as there are now because it was too grassy. If we didn't use the rowboat, we waded through the soft muck and grass to discover what boys like to find. I used to fish Cougar Creek using a telescoping rod. I used mostly wet flies. It was good fishing then. We caught cutthroat out of the creek before the brush and trees were all cut down along the creek in the early 1970s. It ruined the trout habitat. In the spring, everyone fished for catfish. Folks used to burn tires along the shore to attract them. People used to fill bags with them. It was a good place for kids to grow up.

A QUESTIONED CORNER

There have been a number of recognized surveys done near Cougar Bay. The most contentious area involves the line between Sections 21 and 22, roughly the line dividing the bay from its marshy area and the outlet of Cougar Creek. As a local surveyor in Coeur d'Alene, Idaho, I had the experience of working with a disputed surveyed corner of land in Cougar Bay.

In December 1891, Clayton Miller surveyed the line dividing the two sections. He started at the common southern corners of Sections 21 and 22 and measured north. He entered the marsh at a distance of eighteen chains. A surveying chain is sixty-six feet long. At forty chains, he established a midway quarter corner, marking it by digging a pit, burying one stone with "1/4" written on it and piling dirt to form two visible mounds. He continued north, left the marsh and set the northern corner of the sections.

In the late 1940s, William Ashley, the Kootenai County surveyor, looked for Miller's quarter corner but didn't find it and declared it lost. Following the United States General Land Office's rules, Ashley established a new quarter corner at the halfway point and on the original surveyed line but filed no public record. Land surveys were not required to be filed in public records in Idaho until 1978. Surveys were filed with the surveyor, and a copy was given to the owner.

In the early 1980s, John Pointner, owner of land to the east in Section 22, became obsessed with the line dividing his property and Section 21. I had taken over my dad's surveying business, and it happens that he was the county surveyor, so he had kept all the county survey files. John visited my office numerous times to research the survey over a few months. Then, he filed a lawsuit against Earl Johnson, the owner of land to the west in Section 21. Pointer claimed he had found evidence of Miller's original quarter corner. Pointer's corner was some seven hundred feet to the northwest of

Ashley's position. During this time, the Idaho Transportation Department was buying land near this area to construct new U.S. 95.

No local surveyors would accept Pointner's evidence. He then hired a surveyor from Grangeville, Idaho. This surveyor was being investigated by the State Licensing Board, had been told to fix some of his work, not to take on new work and that his license would be revoked. He nevertheless did the survey for Pointner and recorded the new quarter corner in the Kootenai County Public Records. As promised, this surveyor's license was suspended so that by the time the trial took place, he couldn't testify. Pointner hired a replacement who was unfamiliar with the case and legal boundary surveys. At trial, district court judge Prather ruled in favor of Johnson, nullifying Pointner's claim. Pointner appealed to the Idaho Supreme Court, which in 1991 upheld Prather's ruling.

The Johnson family sold its property to Mike McCormack (McCormack Properties of Idaho) in 1993. A few complicated property transactions took place after the sale. McCormack's young surveyor relied on the bogus survey filed with the county, sure that he was right. It was the only survey recorded with the county. During the property line adjustments, McCormack's surveyor was told by someone that Pointer's quarter corner had been legally contested.

McCormack's surveyor came to my office one day, as he knew I was familiar with the dispute. Years before, during another meeting on an unrelated property line question, I told him he would become a good surveyor but only after he stepped in a few buckets of sh*t. At this meeting, after looking over the Supreme Court's decision I had laid out on my desk and realizing his error, McCormack's surveyor asked me if this was one of those buckets. I replied, "Congratulations, you've made your first step."

COUGAR BAY UTOPIA

My family moved to quaint little Coeur d'Alene in 1959. Five years later, we moved to our home at the mouth of Cougar Bay. Our mom called it her "Utopia." Back then, from the Spokane River to the mouth of Cougar Bay, the waters were filled with rafts of logs, which had been floated down the lake to be stored there for the sawmills down the river. These bundles became our playground as we laughed in the face of danger.

Throughout the years, we enjoyed water skiing in the bay long before it was made a no-wake zone. A little seaweed never stopped us, just slowed us down a few times. The log booms and log bundles kept the general public away for fear of hitting a dead-head or two. It seemed like our own private bay. We learned to sail on a little Sunfish in the bay while our parents enjoyed the open waters of the lake on their larger sailboat, *Skoal*, the wind blowing all our cares away. We enjoyed watching the osprey dive for fish in front of the house or the eagles soar high above on the warm air currents. We would paddle our canoe deep into the bay, enjoying the many bird species singing their glorious songs. In the spring, we watched the geese and ducks swim into the dangers of the bay with their babies, coming back later with one or two less every time. In the winter, when the bay froze over, our mom and friends enjoyed ice skating while the boys, both young and old, enjoyed a game or two of hockey. There were times when our friends in Casco Bay would drive a Jeep or snowmobile across the frozen lake either to town or into the bay.

Times have definitely changed. Coeur d'Alene is no longer a quaint little town, and the log booms and log rafts are long gone for our kids or grandkids to climb on. The bay is now a no-wake zone, and there are fewer osprey and eagles. The lake is busier with large boats, their waves trying to chip away the sand once protected by the log booms. But to this day, we can still look out over Lake Coeur d'Alene to the bay and see the timeless beauty and reminisce about the bygone days of our Little Utopia.

MOONLIGHT AT COUGAR BAY

Frogs burble and loudly croak in grassy mud. The full moon's cupped reflection plays on rippling water. A silhouette of honking Canada geese crosses the moon. In the dimming light, wood ducks preen and stretch, perhaps getting ready to roost in the nearby brush. An otter somersaults on the water and disappears. Bats swoop and stitch geometric figures on a violet sky. The great horned owl's hoot echoes in the coming night.

ANOTHER WINTER'S TALE

Scott W. Reed
January 13, 1995
Nickels Worth

Winter can be like the titillating, fictional lover: temperamental, capricious, disturbing with wild swings in mood and then, suddenly, perfectly beautiful and desirable. The novel ends there.

This winter could end with such perfection in the first week of 1995. Local climatologist Cliff Harris tells us that the first four days of the new year made a record for consecutive, cloudless days for winter.

Clear means cold. Fernan Lake froze early; was snowed upon and now freezes with a skateable but rough surface. Fernan becomes the choice place to skate.

Hundreds are out there—a return to those halcyon days of yore. Ever see the photo of Ft. Sherman soldiers and girls on skates by Tubbs Hill looking pleased with what they are doing?

The *Coeur d'Alene Press* touts Fernan with photos and stories. Positive press to push people to find fun in the great outdoors. Will the floating rink substitute for the floating green in the January handouts for the CDA Resort?

City Editor Dave Bond asks me if there should not be a lifeguard on Fernan and then writes an editorial urging county supervision. Ice Control?

Fernan Lake skaters on the rough surface are more likely to need a podiatrist or an orthodontist than a lifeguard.

CHRONOLOGY
OF THE COUGAR BAY BATTLE

Cougar Bay became a nature preserve after a long, drawn-out process that took over a decade of opposition and thousands of dollars spent in legal appeals and fees. It all started in 1992, when a developer from Hawaii proposed building a subdivision along Cougar Bay's northern shore. Environmental activists and entities such as the Friends of Cougar Bay, Rural Kootenai Organization, The Nature Conservancy, the Bureau of Land Management and Kootenai County fought against any development on Cougar Bay. It did not end until 2005, when the final piece of Cougar Bay was secured and made into the Cougar Bay Nature Preserve.

A Timeline of Events Leading to Cougar Bay's Preservation

1992, January to Spring
Mike McCormack, a developer from Hawaii, announced that he had purchased 11.64 acres of the Healy property on the northwest end of Cougar Bay. It included 3,100 feet of waterfront and about 80 acres of lake bottom. McCormack intended to build a seven-house subdivision. The Coeur d'Alene City Council heard from a handful of concerned citizens, including a local bird expert. The council approved the subdivision unanimously. Though McCormack was compelled to present his proposal to

the city council because it was in an area of city impact, its approval meant nothing. The land was within the county's jurisdiction.

1992, Summer

Kootenai County held a series of public hearings on the McCormack proposal. To oppose McCormack Properties' plans at Cougar Bay, the Friends of Cougar Bay, a nonprofit organization, was formed. The Friends collected 2,500 petition signatures at the Kootenai County Fair opposing the development. In August 1992, they organized a flotilla; an array of twenty watercraft floated out in Cougar Bay with large banners saying, "SAVE COUGAR BAY." The Friends continued to unmask the project's flaws, enlist public support and brought the development to a standstill by the fall of 1992. The Friends heard that The Nature Conservancy sometimes bought land and would later sell to government agencies to protect natural and sensitive areas. To seek a solution, Scott Reed, a lawyer who was one of the Friends of Cougar Bay, asked The Nature Conservancy of Idaho to negotiate with McCormack Properties about the possibility of buying the former Healy acreage and shoreland.

1993

In March 1993, the Friends heard that McCormack would sell to The Nature Conservancy—but only if the Friends would remain neutral to his newly proposed upland ninety-two-house development on adjacent property to the west, now the Ridge at Cougar Bay. The Friends agreed. As part of the deal, McCormack also stated that he would "gift" a wildlife sanctuary of some submerged eighty acres in front of the Healy property if the Kootenai County commissioners approved the upland housing development. This was the beginning of a dispute as to whether the state owned submerged land beneath Lake Coeur d'Alene or not.

1994

The Nature Conservancy paid $500,000 to McCormack and acquired the first parcel of key habitat in Cougar Bay, the former Healy shoreline. Ownership of this parcel was later transferred to the Bureau of Land Management for long-term management. This is a non-motorized boat launch area and one of few public access areas on Lake Coeur d'Alene.

After a series of public hearings before the Kootenai County Planning and Zoning Commission and county commissioners in late 1993, the county commissioners approved McCormack's upland proposed ninety-two-house subdivision on 118-acre property overlooking Cougar Bay (the Ridge at Cougar Bay). The property was purchased from the Earl Johnson family. In January 1994, some of the former members of the Friends of Cougar Bay, who had not agreed to individual neutrality, and other concerned citizens formed the Rural Kootenai Organization (RKO) to oppose McCormack's ninety-two-house subdivision plan and to continue to keep Cougar Bay and its surrounding land from being developed. RKO opposed McCormack's Ridge at Cougar Bay by first opposing his proposed waterline delivery for the development. The waterline would tap into water from the Rathdrum Aquifer and run it over Blackwell Hill to reach the development near U.S. 95. The plan was approved by the Department of Lands despite objections from RKO.

1995
McCormack sought to build an aboveground rapid waste disposal infiltration system. RKO opposed this plan, citing the potential for groundwater contamination. However, the Idaho Department of Health and Welfare approved McCormack's rapid waste-water infiltration system by a two-to-one vote.

1996–98
McCormack's once proposed wildlife sanctuary "gift" that lay beneath the lake in front of the former Healy property (now managed by BLM) was challenged by RKO. A lawsuit against the Kootenai County commissioners sought a ruling on the lakebed's ownership. McCormack joined the commissioners' side of the suit as an intervenor. Eventually, the Idaho Supreme Court ruled that the lakebed belonged to the state, not McCormack. The commissioners were ordered to reconsider McCormack's subdivision proposal without the wildlife sanctuary being part of it. They approved it.

1998
The Nature Conservancy of Idaho purchased 88 acres from the Crown Pacific Lumber Company at the head of Cougar Bay, which has become the Cougar Bay Nature Preserve. This was TNC's first permanent acquisition in Kootenai County. The preserve consisted of two parcels (35.5 and 53.1 acres) totaling 88.6 acres purchased for $245,000. Crown Pacific had purchased it from the McAvoy family, explaining the name of the road leading to the nature preserve parking lot.

2000–01

McCormack Properties defaulted on land payments to the Earl Johnson family for the Ridge at Cougar Bay. A sheriff's sale was held in July 2000, and the land was purchased back by the Johnsons. However, McCormack was given one year to redeem the property before it legally went back to them. Starting in July 2001 (the one-year sheriff's sale deadline), the Johnson family granted McCormack Properties a series of extensions as McCormack began negotiating a settlement with Rural Kootenai Organization.

2001, AUGUST

Rural Kootenai Organization, McCormack Properties and Kootenai County negotiated a binding settlement before Idaho Supreme Court justice Gerald Schroeder. McCormack would be allowed to develop a smaller seventy-seven-house subdivision on the northern and western areas of the Earl Johnson land in exchange for granting a thirty-five-acre conservation easement on the properties' lower eastern and southern portions.

2001, FALL

The Inland Northwest Land Trust negotiated the terms of the thirty-five-acre conservation agreement with McCormack Properties.

2002

McCormack Properties sold the Ridge at Cougar Bay property to developer Bill Radobanko, who was also bound by the negotiated conservation easement settlement.

2003

The Bureau of Land Management, with the help of Kootenai County, purchased 150-plus acres at Cougar Bay that is a mixture of waterfront, marsh and timberland from John Pointner. It was a creative contract that called for the Bureau of Land Management and Kootenai County to pay Pointner $5,000 a month until his death. After that, Pointner would forgive the debt and Cougar Bay and the surrounding hillside would be forever protected from becoming yet another upscale housing development. Pointner died twenty-five months after the deal was signed, which means he received a total of $125,000 from the two government agencies.

This land is located near the two earlier conservation acquisitions in Cougar Bay, the former Healy shoreland property and The Nature Conservancy's eighty-eight-acre property. It's a significant purchase since nearly 90 percent of Coeur d'Alene Lake's shoreline is privately owned. John Pointner wanted the trails around Cougar Bay named after him. Today, the trail is called the John Pointner Memorial Wildlife Sanctuary Trail.

2021

In 2021, the Bureau of Land Management purchased the Cougar Bay Nature Preserve from The Nature Conservancy (88.51 acres). The BLM utilized $1.6 million from the Land and Water Conservation Fund to complete the transaction. The acquisition expands the 155-acre John C. Pointner Memorial Sanctuary. The area had been co-managed by the BLM and The Nature Conservancy.

A SHORT TIMELINE OF THE NATURE CONSERVANCY'S EFFORT ON COUGAR BAY

1994, FEBRUARY

A group of concerned citizens, environmental groups and neighboring landowners objected to a proposed development on the shoreline of Cougar Bay. The Nature Conservancy was asked to help negotiate a solution with the owner of the planned development, McCormack Properties of Idaho. TNC received $5,000 from Foundation Northwest to aid its Cougar Bay preservation project.

1994, MARCH

The Nature Conservancy acquired 11.64 acres from McCormack Properties of Idaho, including 3,000 feet of lake frontage. At the time, McCormack Properties quitclaimed 68.8 acres to the State of Idaho in order to clarify an issue regarding ownership of lands under 2,128 feet, the high-water mark.

1994, APRIL

The Nature Conservancy closed on the sale of the 11.64-acre parcel to the Bureau of Land Management. It is now a popular motorless boat launching area.

1998, MAY

The Nature Conservancy purchased two parcels (33.5 and 53.1 acres) totaling 88.6 acres for $245,000 from Crown Pacific. TNC partnered with the BLM to maintain the area as a nature preserve.

2005, JUNE
The Nature Conservancy acquired an additional 2.06 acres adjacent to the Crown Pacific property as a gift from the Earl Johnson family.

2014
Hiking trails were built along the shore of Cougar Bay Nature Preserve by volunteers. A lookout platform was also constructed by a Post Falls Boy Scout troop.

2021
The Bureau of Land Management purchased the Cougar Bay Nature Preserve from The Nature Conservancy (88.51 acres). The BLM now manages the entire Cougar Bay Nature Preserve.

APPENDIX C

JOHN POINTNER'S NEWSPAPER ADVERTISEMENT

Advertisement

Obituary of Cougar Bay Marsh

By John C. Pointner

Cougar Bay Marsh, heart of the environment, is owned by John Pointner. It is healthy because I have taken care of it. Without the marsh, environmentally speaking, the area would be like a picture frame without a picture. Hillsides surrounding a stinking cesspool mud flat would have existed for twenty years if I had not prevented it. The Cougar Bay watershed embraces twelve thousand acres. The national average of siltation washout is nine tons per acre per year. Assuming these figures are correct Cougar Bay receives one hundred and eight thousand tons of sediment pollution per year. Cougar Creek has been reported as exceeding the average. For twenty years my Delta Control canals have removed enough of this massive pollution load from the marsh to restore it. It is illogical to give great consideration to controlling the pittance of highway storm water run off crossing McCormack's proposed homesites while disregarding the largest problem. McCormack's proposed development and others on the hillside hold the financial key to controlling the major pollution damage to the marsh. The tax base is increased by each new structure. New and all existing ownerships within the entire watershed of Cougar Gulch must be formed into a local taxing District with these monies devoted to creating an aquatic wildlife park, nurturing, improving and preserving the marsh. Without a healthy marsh Cougar Bay has no environmental value.

In late 1960's and early 1970's watershed pollutants and siltation were flushed out of Cougar Gulch in huge quantities killing one half of the vegetation of Cougar Bay Marsh. Cyanide formed in nature killing all living things except the worms and bugs. At my request North Idaho College chemically tested the marsh area over a three year period furnishing me their reports. The University of Idaho tested and reported the algae to be of the green type. If it had been blue-green type the area could not have been restored. The Alpha Medical Laboratory gave me a six page scientific analysis and up-dated it ten years later, commending me for my work in restoring the marsh. Senator James McClure obtained Wisconsin's Upper Great Lakes Demonstration Project Research Documents for me, this stacked six inches high. Correlating all information I engineered and designed a canal and settling basin system. I could not complete this "Delta Control" system because of proliferation of new laws and regulations I managed to legally construct enough of this system to save the marsh. First over a period of two winters dynamite expert Gregory Nearpass and I placed ditching dynamite eighteen inches apart for four thousand feet using one ton of explosives. We waded in deep mud that stunk like a cesspool, which it was! This preliminary ditch three feet deep, six feet wide and four thousand feet long temporarily diverted the pollutant siltation flow away from the heavily destroyed grass land area allowing it to recover. With my hydraulic dredge I dredged a fifteen foot deep large settling basin near my buildings. With a large backhoe of Fritz Kindler Construction Co., and my rebuilt, low down pressure bulldozer, we excavated a settling basin along the South hillside six hundred feet long, one hundred feet wide and ten feet deep. I then rough bulldozed a canal for one thousand feet along the hillside edge. I bulldozed a sixty feet wide five foot deep canal for one quarter of a mile South from my buildings. I was never able to properly connect this canal to the North settling basin because a new government regulation required transportation of all excavated material removed from below 2128 ft. elevation to remote high ground. Due to this restrictive regulation I have never been able to complete enlargement of the very important Southern one quarter mile of the North South diversion canal to keep the watershed siltation pollutants from overflowing and damaging the major vegetated area. Only the preliminary dynamite ditch provides partial protection with the result that over flowing nutrients have created a huge under water weed bed mass out-bound from the marsh. This weed bed now restricts oxygen laden fresh water inflow. Before the weed bed formed wind induced tide like water level fluctuation of two inches in twelve hours replaced oxygen depleted water with oxygen rich water from the lake. Oxygen is required to nurture the marsh.

If the canals I built are not cleaned out and lengthened lakeward beyond the underwater weed bed to restore tidal flow the marsh will become anaerobic again and die from this cause. The one quarter mile, sixty feet wide, five feet deep canal has collected silt and pollutants until it is only five inches deep. The bullhead fishermen have given up trying to catch fish in it because there is no water for the fish to swim in. My canal and settling basis system saved the marsh preventing it from becoming a mud flat twenty years ago. Because foolish laws and regulations prevented me from completing the system the excavated components have improperly filled making the system ineffective. All that is required to completely destroy Cougar Bay Marsh now that my incomplete Delta Control System has filled is to have a heavy snow pack about four feet high from Cougar Bay to Mica Peak then one week of warm mid-winter rain and the massive pollutant out wash from loose earth, overflowed septic systems, barn yards etc., will rush down out of Cougar Gulch. This time it will completely kill the marsh. No vegetation or wildlife will be left alive only a barren stinking mud flat cesspool will remain.

At the age of seventy-three years I do not have the physical strength or money to continue paying government two or three dollars for permits for every dollar to do the actual work. Therefore, I suggest that a taxing district be formed to impose taxes upon all Cougar Gulch watershed ownerships. These monies must be used to renovate and complete the "Delta Control" protection of Cougar Bay Marsh resulting in and maintaining a well cared for aquatic wildlife park. McCormack's sub-division including other new construction and ownerships will add to that tax base. With my thirty years engineering ownership experience I will advise how the Marsh can be saved. Someone else has to do the work and finance it. Cougar Bay is a suburban area surrounded by people adversely impacting the marsh. Any attempt to treat it as a wilderness area to be left alone will destroy it. Its only hope for continued environmental viability is to protect the marsh as a well cared for Aquatic Wildlife Park with no encroachment by man in the wetland other than to enhance and protect it. I have done the job for thirty years. I know how to do it. Now let someone else do it. For the next one hundred years.

John C. Pointner-B.S. Mechanical Engineer
University of Idaho, 1947
P.O. Box 54
Coeur d'Alene, Idaho 83814

Courtesy Coeur d'Alene Press.

PLANT SPECIES OF COUGAR BAY

Plant Species List
Location: Cougar Bay, John C. Pointner Memorial Wildlife Sanctuary
Provided by LeAnn Abell, BLM Botanist

TREES

Common Name	Scientific Name
grand fir	*Abies grandis*
water birch	*Betula occidentalis*
paper birch	*Betula papyrifera*
western larch	*Larix occidentalis*
lodgepole pine	*Pinus contorta*
western white pine	*Pinus monticola*
ponderosa pine	*Pinus ponderosa*
quaking aspen	*Populus tremuloides*
black cottonwood	*Populus trichocarpa*
Douglas fir	*Pseudotsuga menziesii*

SHRUBS

Common Name	Scientific Name
Rocky Mountain maple	*Acer glabrum*
thinleaf alder	*Alnus incana*
red alder	*Alnus rubra*
serviceberry	*Amelanchier alnifolia*
Cascade Oregon grape	*Berberis nervosa*
creeping Oregon grape	*Berberis repens*
black hawthorn	*Crataegus douglasii*
oceanspray	*Holodiscus discolor*
twinflower	*Linnaea borealis*
orange honeysuckle	*Lonicera ciliosa*
bearberry honeysuckle	*Lonicera involucrata*
Utah honeysuckle	*Lonicera utahensis*
pachistima	*Paxistima myrsinites*
syringa	*Philadelphus lewisii*
mallow ninebark	*Physocarpus malvaceus*
baldhip rose	*Rosa gymnocarpa*
thimbleberry	*Rubus parviflorus*
blue elderberry	*Sambucus cerulea*
shiny-leaf spiraea	*Spiraea betulifolia*
hardhack	*Spiraea douglasii*
common snowberry	*Symphoricarpos alba*

WILDFLOWERS

Common Name	Scientific Name
yarrow	*Achillea millefolium*
baneberry	*Actaea rubra*
trail-plant, pathfinder	*Adenocaulon bicolor*
pearly everlasting	*Anaphalis margaritacea*

Left: View of Cougar Bay. *Bureau of Land Management.*

Below: Cinnamon teal ducks in Cougar Bay. *Courtesy Roberta Rich.*

Western painted turtle on log. *Courtesy Roberta Rich.*

Osprey with fish at Cougar Bay. *Courtesy Darren Clark, Idahobirds.net.*

Cougar Bay trail terrain. *The Nature Conservancy.*

Huckleberries on a bush.
Courtesy of Northwest Wild Foods.

Left: Drawing of an osprey. *Illustration © Christine Marie Larsen.*

Below: Osprey with fish. *Courtesy of Jim Ekins, University of Idaho Extension.*

Above: Osprey on nest at Cougar Bay. *Courtesy of Jim Ekins, University of Idaho Extension.*

Left: Annual osprey cruise with wildlife expert. *Courtesy of Jim Ekins, University of Idaho Extension.*

Cougar Bay wetland. *The Nature Conservancy.*

The Ridge at Cougar Bay entrance. *Author's collection.*

Cougar Bay trail. *The Nature Conservancy.*

Allis-Chalmers bulldozer. *Courtesy of Roberta Rich.*

Aurora Winter. Painting by Wes Hanson.

Soft Sunrise. Painting by Wes Hanson.

Above: Swamp buggy.
Author's collection.

Left: Cougar Bay trail.
Courtesy of Roberta Rich.

John C. Pointner Memorial Wildlife Sanctuary Trail

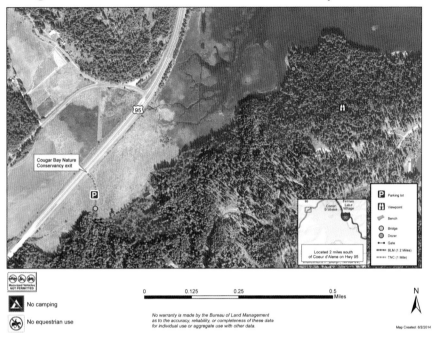

Map of John C. Pointner Memorial Trail. *Bureau of Land Management.*

A visitor at a Cougar Bay trail marker. *Author's collection.*

Above: Eagle at Cougar Bay. *Courtesy of Cara Anthony at Cougar Bay Lodge.*

Left: Cougar Bay calm waters. *Courtesy of Roberta Rich.*

Left: Cougar Bay
Nature Preserve sign
on the highway. *Author's
collection.*

Below: Cougar Bay
shoreline edge. *Courtesy
of Roberta Rich.*

Bay Moon. Painting by Wes Hanson.

windflower	*Anemone piperi*
bigleaf sandwort	*Antennaria macrophylla*
heartleaf arnica	*Arnica cordifolia*
wild ginger	*Asarum caudatum*
showy aster	*Aster conspicuus*
dwarf enchanter's, nightshade	*Circaea alpine*
queen-cup bead-lily	*Clintonia uniflora*
blue-eyed mary	*Collinsia parviflora*
Hooker fairy-bells	*Disporum hookeri*
glacier lily	*Erythronium grandiflorum*
woodland strawberry	*Fragaria vesca*
mountain strawberry	*Fragaria virginiana*
sweet-scented bedstraw	*Galium triflorum*
round-leaf alumroot	*Heuchera cylindrica*
white-flowered hawkweed	*Hieracium albiflorum*
common tarweed	*Madia gracilis*
side-flowered mitrewort	*Mitella stauropetala*
broad-leaved montia	*Montia cordifolia*
mountain sweet, cicely	*Osmorhiza chilensis*
self-heal	*Prunella vulgaris*
starry false Solomon's seal	*Smilacina stellata*
western meadowrue	*Thalictrum occidentale*
white trillium	*Trillium ovatum*
pioneer violet	*Viola glabella*

GRASSES AND GRASS-LIKE PLANTS

Common Name	Scientific Name
Columbia brome	*Bromus vulgaris*
pinegrass	*Calamagrostis rubescens*
lens sedge	*Carex lenticularis*
blue wildrye	*Elymus glaucus*

Ferns

Common Name	Scientific Name
brittle bladder-fern	*Cystopteris fragilis*
male fern	*Dryopteris filix-mas*
common swordfern	*Polystichum munitum*
bracken fern	*Pteridium aquilinum*

Nonnative Plants

Common Name	Scientific Name
smooth brome	*Bromus inermis*
bachelor buttons	*Centaurea cyanus*
spotted knapweed	*Centaurea maculosa*
ox-eye daisy	*Chrysanthemum leucanthemum*
Canada thistle	*Cirsium arvense*
bull thistle	*Cirsium vulgare*
orchardgrass	*Dactylis glomerata*
common St. John's wort	*Hypericum perforatum*
reed canarygrass	*Phalaris arundinacea*
timothy	*Phleum pratense*
sulphur cinquefoil	*Potentilla recta*
creeping buttercup	*Ranunculus repens*
sheep sorrel	*Rumex acetosella*
curly dock	*Rumex crispus*
climbing nightshade	*Solanum dulcamara*
common tansy	*Tanacetum vulgare*
common dandelion	*Taraxacum officinale*
yellow salsify	*Tragopogon dubius*
yellow clover	*Trifolium aureum*
alsike clover	*Trifolium hybridum*
red clover	*Trifolium pratense*
ventenata	*Ventenata dubia*

BIRDS OF COUGAR BAY

Lake Coeur d'Alene, Cougar Bay
Kootenai, Idaho, US
ebird.org/hotspot/L834075
150 species (+9 other taxa), year-round, all years

This checklist is generated with data from eBird (ebird.org), a global database of bird sightings from birders like you. If you enjoy this checklist, please consider contributing your sightings to eBird. It is 100 percent free to take part, and your observations will help support birders, researchers and conservationists worldwide.

WATERFOWL

American wigeon
Barrow's goldeneye
blue-winged teal
bufflehead
cackling goose
Canada goose
canvasback
cinnamon teal
common/Barrow's goldeneye
common goldeneye
common merganser
domestic goose sp. (domestic type)
duck sp.
Eurasian wigeon
gadwall
greater/lesser scaup
greater scaup
green-winged teal
hooded merganser
lesser scaup
long-tailed duck
mallard
northern pintail
northern shoveler

red-breasted merganser
redhead
ring-necked duck
ruddy duck
scoter sp.
snow goose
surf scoter
trumpeter swan
trumpeter/tundra swan
tufted duck
tundra swan
white-winged scoter
wood duck

GROUSE, QUAIL AND ALLIES
California quail
wild turkey

GREBES
eared grebe
horned grebe
pied-billed grebe
red-necked grebe
western grebe

PIGEONS AND DOVES
Eurasian collared-dove
mourning dove
rock pigeon

HUMMINGBIRDS
black-chinned hummingbird
calliope hummingbird

RAILS, GALLINULES AND ALLIES
American coot

SHOREBIRDS
greater yellowlegs
killdeer
lesser yellowlegs
solitary sandpiper
spotted sandpiper
Wilson's phalarope
Wilson's snipe

GULLS, TERNS AND SKIMMERS
Bonaparte's gull
California gull
Caspian tern
common tern
Forster's tern
glaucous gull
gull sp.
herring gull
Iceland gull
lesser black-backed gull
ring-billed gull
short-billed gull

LOONS
common loon
red-throated loon

CORMORANTS AND ANHINGAS
double-crested cormorant

PELICANS
American white pelican

HERONS, IBIS AND ALLIES
great blue heron

VULTURES, HAWKS AND ALLIES
bald eagle
northern harrier
osprey
red-tailed hawk
sharp-shinned hawk
turkey vulture

KINGFISHERS
belted kingfisher

WOODPECKERS
downy woodpecker
hairy woodpecker
northern flicker
pileated woodpecker
red-naped sapsucker

FALCONS AND CARACARAS
American kestrel
merlin
peregrine falcon

TYRANT FLYCATCHERS: PEWEES, KINGBIRDS AND ALLIES
cordilleran flycatcher
eastern kingbird
Hammond's flycatcher
western wood-pewee
willow flycatcher

VIREOS
Cassin's vireo
red-eyed vireo
warbling vireo

SHRIKES
northern shrike

JAYS, MAGPIES, CROWS AND RAVENS
American crow
black-billed magpie
Canada jay
common raven
Steller's jay

TITS, CHICKADEES AND TITMICE
black-capped chickadee
chestnut-backed chickadee
chickadee sp.
mountain chickadee

MARTINS AND SWALLOWS
bank swallow
barn swallow
cliff swallow
northern rough-winged swallow
swallow sp.
tree swallow
violet-green swallow

KINGLETS
golden-crowned kinglet
ruby-crowned kinglet

NUTHATCHES
pygmy nuthatch
red-breasted nuthatch
white-breasted nuthatch

TREECREEPERS
brown creeper

WRENS
Bewick's wren
marsh wren
Pacific wren

Starlings and Mynas
European starling

Catbirds, Mockingbirds and Thrashers
gray catbird

Thrushes
American robin
Swainson's thrush
western bluebird

Waxwings
bohemian waxwing
cedar waxwing

Old-World Sparrows
house sparrow

Finches, Euphonias and Allies
American goldfinch
Cassin's finch
common redpoll
evening grosbeak
house finch
pine siskin
red crossbill

New-World Sparrows
chipping sparrow
dark-eyed junco
savannah sparrow
song sparrow
spotted towhee
white-crowned sparrow

Blackbirds
Brewer's blackbird
Bullock's oriole
crown-headed cowbird
red-winged blackbird
yellow-headed blackbird

Wood-Warblers
American redstart
common yellowthroat
Nashville warbler
orange-crowned warbler
Townsend's warbler
Wilson's warbler
yellow-rumped warbler
yellow warbler

Cardinals, Grosbeaks and Allies
black-headed grosbeak
western tanager

GEOLOGICAL TOUR OF COUGAR BAY

The Geological Society of America Field Guide 41
Pre-Belt basement tour: Late Archean–Early Proterozoic rocks of the
Cougar Gulch area, southern Priest River complex, Idaho
Andrew M. Buddington Science Department, Spokane Community
College, 1810 Greene Street, Spokane, Washington 99217, USA
Da Wang Earth Sciences, School of the Environment, Washington State
University, P.O. Box 642812, Pullman, Washington 99164, USA
P. Ted Doughty PRISEM Geoscience Consulting, 823 West 25th Avenue,
Spokane, Washington 99203, USA

ABSTRACT

The Cougar Gulch area near Coeur d'Alene, Idaho, is a newly recognized Paleoproterozoic to Archean basement occurrence located in the southern Priest River complex. Here, a structural culmination exposes deeper levels of the core complex infrastructure, similar to where Archean basement is exposed in the northern portion of the complex near Priest River, Idaho. At Cougar Gulch, the basement rocks are composed of a variety of granitic orthogneisses and amphibolite, which are unconformably overlain by a graphite-bearing orthoquartzite. The orthoquartzite is in turn overlain by the Hauser Lake Gneiss. The similarity of structure, metamorphic fabrics, and kinematics here and in the northern portions of the complex is consistent with the Cougar Gulch area being the southern continuation of the Spokane dome mylonite zone.

Neoarchean amphibolites (2.65 Ga) have been identified as part of the basement sequence. These amphibolites had a basaltic protolith and can be distinguished geochemically from amphibolites found within the overlying Hauser Lake Gneiss (Mesoproterozoic, Lower Belt Group equivalent), which are metamorphosed Moyie sills. The Archean amphibolites have steeper REE (rare earth element) slopes and consistently higher REE values. Protoliths of the Paleoproterozoic orthogneisses (1.87–1.86 Ga) are calc-alkaline, "I-type" monzogranites and granodiorites, which exhibit subduction-related geochemical characteristics such as high LILE:HFSE (large ion lithophile element: high field strength element) concentrations, along with characteristic depletions in Nb, Ta, P, Ti, and Eu. A second distinctive geochemical unit of orthogneiss, the Kidd Creek tonalite, exhibits TTG (tonalite-trondhjemite-granodiorite) geochemical characteristics. The Kidd Creek tonalite has Sr/Y and La/Yb ratios, along with Y and HREE (heavy rare earth element) concentrations (no Eu anomalies) similar to Precambrian TTG compositions formed in subduction settings. Detrital zircon data from the orthoquartzite unit, along with characteristic graphite and its consistent stratigraphic level support correlation to the pre–Belt Gold Cup Quartzite in the northern part of the complex.

NOTES

1. Figure 3 from A.M. Buddington, D. Wang and P.T. Doughty, 2016, "Pre-Belt Basement Tour: Late Archean–Early Proterozoic Rocks of the Cougar Gulch Area, Southern Priest River Complex, Idaho," in *Exploring the Geology of the Inland Northwest: Geological Society of America Field Guide* 41, edited by R.S. Lewis and K.L. Schmidt, 265–84, doi.org/10.1130/2016.0041(09). Copyright © The Geological Society of America. Used with permission.
2. Idaho Fish and Game, idfg.idaho.gov/science.
3. Coeur d'Alene tribe, www.cdatribe-nsn.gov/our-tribe/tribal-lands.
4. Museum of North Idaho, museumni.org/blog.
5. Idaho Fish and Game, idfg.idaho.gov/conservation/wetlands.
6. Idaho Fish and Game, idfg.idaho.gov/press/bald-eagles-doing-well.
7. Ric Clarke, "City Oks Wetlands Housing," *Coeur d'Alene Press*, July 23, 1992.
8. David Bond, "Cougar Bay Friends Vow to Fight," *Coeur d'Alene Press*, August 12, 1992.
9. Mike McLean, "Foley Goes to Bat for Land Swap," *Coeur d'Alene Press*, September 28, 1993.
10. Reina Sheres, "BLM Airs Plans, Hears Concerns," *Coeur d'Alene Press*, July 14, 1994.
11. *Rural Kootenai Organization, Inc., and Linda Erickson v. Board of County Commissioners, Kootenai County, State of Idaho, and McCormack Properties of Idaho*, 99.26 ISCR1054, 1999.

12. Idaho Coalition of Land Trusts, www.idaholandtrusts.org/conservation-easements.

13. Idaho Code 55-2101.

14. Inland N.W. Land Conservancy, inlandnwland.org.

15. Coeur d'Alene Management Plan 2009, www2.deq.idaho.gov/admin/LEIA/api/document/download/11122.

16. Idaho Fish and Game, idfg.idaho.gov/old-web/docs/wildlife/nongame/leafletWetlands.PDF.

17. Scott Forsell, interview by Theresa Shaffer, 2022.

18. Chris Bonsignore, manager of Ducks Unlimited, interview by Theresa Shaffer, 2023.

19. Restoration Partnership, Cougar Bay Wetlands Enhancement Project, www.restorationpartnership.org/Cougar_Bay_Wetlands_project.html.

20. Rob Tiedemann, Mitigation Plan for the McAvoy Fill, Cougar Bay, Coeur d'Alene Lake, Idaho Transportation Department, 1986.

21. Idaho Department of Lands Submerged Land Lease, www.idl.idaho.gov/lakes-rivers/submerged-land-lease/north-idaho-maritime-coeur-dalene-lake-cougar-bay.

ABOUT THE AUTHOR

Theresa Shaffer is a longtime supporter of land conservancy. She lives on a 160-acre original homestead with her life partner. This mostly forested land is protected from development through a conservation easement monitored by a land trust. The Cougar Bay Nature Preserve has been a favorite hiking spot and respite for her for years. Shaffer believes the preserve should have its own story since it took a thirteen-year battle to keep its wild and natural state. She is a retired educator and administrator from the University of Idaho, where she received a master's degree. She has been published in various journals and publications. This is her first book.

Visit us at
www.historypress.com
....